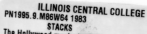
**Illinois Central College
Learning Resources Center**

THE
HOLLYWOOD MUSICAL
GOES TO WAR

THE
HOLLYWOOD MUSICAL
GOES TO WAR

Allen L. Woll

Nelson-Hall nh Chicago

LIBRARY OF CONGRESS CATALOGING IN PUBLICATION DATA

Woll, Allen L.
  The Hollywood musical goes to war.

  Bibliography: p.
  Filmography: p.
  Includes index.
  1. Moving-pictures, Musical—United States—
History and criticism.   2. World War, 1939-1945—
Moving-pictures and the war.   I. Title.
PN1995.9.M86W64   782.81'0973   82-6498
ISBN 0-88229-704-X (cloth)   AACR2
ISBN 0-88229-811-9 (paper)

Manufactured in the United States of America

10 9 8 7 6 5 4 3 2 1

The paper in this book is pH neutral (acid-free).

To Uncle Sam

Contents

Introduction

It is ironic that the musical has been one of Hollywood's most popular film genres and at the same time, one of its most maligned. During the most critical periods of our nation's history the musical film has thrived, apparently in response to the audience's desire for escape from the reality of everyday life.

The first golden age of the film musical coincided with the Great Depression. As millions of people experienced poverty, hunger, and unemployment, Fred Astaire and Ginger Rogers danced across American screens without a care in the world. At the same time, Busby Berkeley and the Warner Brothers' Gold Diggers presented an image of musical opulence which provided a dark parody of actual conditions in the early 1930s. As the sense of national crisis began to ebb with the upturn in the American economy, the film musical virtually disappeared. By 1939 musical production hit new lows.

The musical regained its former glory when the United States entered World War II. By 1944 studios released more than seventy-five song-and-dance films, thus establishing the musical as the dominant film genre of wartime Hollywood. Judy Garland, Betty Grable, Carmen Miranda,

Gene Kelly, Alice Faye, Frank Sinatra, Danny Kaye, and many other stars entertained homefront audiences as fathers, husbands, and sons fought to preserve America's freedom.

The musical has seemingly fulfilled the role of national cheerleader, buoying the spirits of a society beset by war or economic distress. The parade of beautiful dancing girls and lilting melodies apparently allowed the viewer to forget contemporary problems for a few brief hours in the fantasy world of the darkened theatre. The ad campaign for the recent M-G-M musical compilation film *That's Entertainment* (1974) reflected this notion as it offered relief to a public troubled by both Vietnam and Watergate with the catch phrase, "Boy, do we need it now!" The film succeeded beyond the producers' wildest dreams.

This curious social function of the musical film has led critics to dismiss the genre as a frivolous form of escapist art. Blissfully ignoring a nation in peril, the musical served as a musical opiate which caused viewers to forget about their problems rather than do something about them.[1]

The curse of social irrelevance has plagued the Hollywood musical from the days of *The Jazz Singer* to the present, and, as a result, critics have virtually ignored it. For example, a recent study of motion pictures of the Depression devoted a mere three pages to the musical, although it was one of the most popular and profitable genres of this period.[2]

But the frivolous reputation of the musical film is not entirely deserved. It is like the glamorous showgirl who frequented the backstage musicals of the 1930s. Although catty gossip tarnished her image, people began to realize the stories were untrue once they got to know her. Beneath that glittering and forbidding exterior there inevitably beat a heart of gold. The musical film has the same capacity to dazzle and distract, as the costumes, the music, and dance can conceal a serious core.

Critics have often failed to look beneath the glittering facade of the Hollywood musical, and, as a result, they have emphasized the escapist nature of these films. The musicals of the second World War reveal the fallacy of their argument. Between 1941 and 1945, the film musical achieved its greatest popularity and its greatest relevance. Betty Grable's legs, Dorothy Lamour's sarong, and Veronica Lake's hairstyle provided the glamor which disguised a musical comedy with a political commitment. After Pearl Harbor, winning the war became the number one priority of the musical film, as escapism swiftly became an impossibility.

PART ONE

HOLLYWOOD GOES TO WAR

1

A Committed Entertainment

Hollywood entered the second World War almost three years before Washington, D. C. While the nation wavered between a sympathy for our European friends and a mistrust of outright intervention, film studios released a "flock of features to whip up enthusiasm for preparedness and the draft." *Variety*, the show business oracle, noted the trend almost immediately and dubbed the new films "preparedness pix." By the end of 1940 film schedules were hastily revised to include thirty-six titles concerning "conscription, flying, and other phases of war and defense." With such films as *I Married a Nazi, Sergeant York*, and *British Intelligence*, Hollywood assumed an interventionist stance.[1]

Hollywood's definitive commitment to the European war was looked on less fondly in the halls of Congress where isolationist forces, led by Senator Gerald Nye of North Dakota, had not yet been stilled. The so-called patriotism of Hollywood war films became mere propaganda in the eyes of those legislators who believed that the United States should avoid the terrors of war and leave European nations to fight their own battles. As a result, a subcommittee of the Interstate Commerce Commission met in September, 1941, to investigate "Motion Picture Screen and Radio Propaganda."[2]

This investigation reflected Washington's long-standing distrust of the cinematic medium. The preponderant influence of the motion pictures in matters of morals had long been recognized, but not until the 1930s had fears erupted concerning the political uses of film. The Roosevelt Administration's use of the documentary film to support such projects as the Tennessee Valley Authority angered Congressional opponents who began to understand the political implications of the cinema. By 1941 these initial fears escalated to anger as the hearings swiftly revealed.[3]

Senator Nye, the Committee's second witness, saw the presence of a vast conspiracy urging American entry into the war. Nye contended that screen propaganda was the most insidious of all: "Arriving at the theatre, Mr. and Mrs. America sit, with guard completely down, mind open, ready and eager for entertainment. In that frame of mind they follow through the story which the screen tells. If, somewhere in that story there is planted a narrative, a speech, or a declaration by a favorite actor or actress which seems to pertain to causes which are upsetting so much of the world today, there is planted in the heart and in the mind a feeling, a sympathy, or a distress which is not easily eliminated." He added that the public knew and expected propaganda from newspapers, but motion pictures took the audience completely by surprise. Nye placed blame for this mysterious conspiracy on Jewish interventionist interests. Although the Senator prefaced his comments with a perfunctory "some of my best friends are Jews," he repeatedly criticized Jewish radio commentators, columnists, and publishers for their attempt to deceive the American people.

Senator Bennett C. Clark of Missouri agreed with his colleague's charges, and specifically condemned the film industry for the dissemination of interventionist propaganda. He contended that "not one word on the side of the argument against the war is heard." This was due to the "fact that the moving picture industry is a monopoly controlled by a half dozen men dominated by hatred, who are determined in order to wreak vengeance on Adolf Hitler, a ferocious beast, to plunge this nation into war on behalf of another ferocious beast." Clark's list of those in charge of the film media included Nicholas Schenck, Darryl F. Zanuck, Alexander Korda, and Henry Luce, who was responsible for the "March of Time" series, which "poisons the minds of the American people to go to war."

Clark found fuel for this argument in a government study of theatrical booking practices which investigated the motion picture industry and found a monopolistic situation. Eight major companies (Paramount, Loew's, RKO, Warner Brothers, Twentieth Century-Fox, Columbia, Universal, and United Artists) dominated the business. This situation caused Clark to fear that Hollywood moguls had gained complete control of the media in America.

While Clark and Nye found supposed evidence for their cause in this government report, their talent as film critics was found lacking. Nye in particular saw few of the films in question and the ones he did see he was unable to recall. Senator Ernest McFarland searched Nye's recent speech in St. Louis for all references to objectionable films:

SEN. MCFARLAND:	Did you see *Convoy?*
SEN. NYE:	I think I did.
SEN. MCFARLAND:	Do you remember anything in that picture that was particularly objectionable?
SEN. NYE:	I am at a loss to call to mind any particular feature about it that led me to draw the conclusion which I have drawn.

Nye then admitted that he did not see *Flight Command* (1941), *That Hamilton Woman* (1941), or *Sergeant York* (1941). He was unable to differentiate between *Confessions of a Nazi Spy* and *I Married a Spy* ("For the life of me I could not tell you which was which"). The only film Nye remembered was Charlie Chaplin's *The Great Dictator*, which he claimed was a "portrayal by a great artist, not a citizen of our country . . . that could not do other than build within the heart and mind of those who watched it something of a hatred, detestation of conditions and of leadership that existed abroad."

Wendell L. Willkie, at that time with the Washington law firm of Willkie, Owen, Otis, and Bailly, supported Hollywood's interests before the Committee. Unlike other investigations of the activities of the motion picture industry, representatives of Hollywood presented their positions with valiant fervor, and made no attempt to hide the attitudes that caused them to make films favoring American entry into the war. Willkie sent a letter to Clark before the investigation began. He believed that the Committee sought to inquire whether the motion picture industry, as a whole, and its leading executives, as individuals, were opposed to the Nazi dictatorship in Germany. If this were the case, reasoned Willkie, there need not be an investigation, for "the motion picture industry and its executives *are* opposed to the Hitler regime in Germany."

Willkie explained that the attitude of the film industry represented the "great overwhelming majority of the people of our country." Indeed, Hollywood was just following the opinions of the nation. He contended that the "motion picture industry, like other American industries, is composed of sincere, patriotic citizens." These men admit that the industry "gladly and with great pride, has done all in its power to present to the American public a picture of our Army, our Navy, our Air Corps, and their equipment."

Nevertheless, Willkie explained that Hollywood was accomplishing this task on its own volition, and not at the behest or with the assistance of the current administration. Indeed, "the motion picture industry would be ashamed if it were not doing voluntarily what it is now doing in the national defense."

Willkie also decried the anti-Semitic attitudes of the isolationist forces. He noted that the industry included "Nordics and non-Nordics, Jews and Gentiles, Protestants, Catholics, and native and foreign born." This demonstrates, added Willkie, that "the motion picture industry despises the racial discrimination of nazi-ism and is devoted to the cause of human freedom both in this country and abroad."

Willkie called a long and distinguished list of important Hollywood representatives to lend credence to his arguments. Harry M. Warner, then president of Warner Brothers, was one of the first witnesses. Warner presented his position as unequivocally as possible:

> I am opposed to nazi-ism. I abhor and detest every principle and practice of the Nazi movement. To me, nazi-ism typifies the very opposite of the kind of life every decent man, woman, and child wants to live. I believe nazi-ism is a world revolution whose ultimate objective is to destroy our democracy, wipe out all religion, and enslave our people—just as Germany has destroyed and enslaved Poland, Belgium, Holland, and France. I am ready to give myself and all my personal resources to aid in the defeat of the Nazi menace to the American people.

Warner then explained that his firm produced a wide variety of entertainment films designed to give the public what it wanted to see. He then presented detailed descriptions of *Confessions of a Nazi Spy, Sergeant York, Underground,* and *International Squadron,* by which he hoped to convince the Committee that his films were based solely on fact, as recorded in the daily newspapers, and were therefore not spurious attempts at propaganda.

Darryl F. Zanuck, then vice-president in charge of production at Twentieth Century-Fox, followed Warner on the witness stand. He detailed his Methodist background in Wahoo, Nebraska, (population 891) and recounted his adventures in the U. S. Army during World War I, where he rose to the rank of private first class. His testimony followed that of Warner's fairly closely. Zanuck explained: "In the time of acute national peril, I feel that it is the duty of every American to give his complete cooperation and support to our President and our Congress to do everything to defeat Hitler and preserve America. If this course of necessity leads to war, I want to follow my President along that course."

Zanuck's testimony met with stirring applause from the Senate audience, as he explained that pictures are so "strong and powerful that they sold the American way of life, not only to America, but to the entire world. They sold it so strongly that when dictators took over Italy and Germany, what did Hitler and his flunky, Mussolini, do? The first thing they did was to ban our pictures, throw us out. They wanted no part of the American way of life."

The Committee moved to recess after testimony from Barney Balaban, president of Paramount Pictures. The Committee never resumed its meetings. A small column in the *New York Times* announced its demise, since, after the bombing of Pearl Harbor, the isolationist position swiftly dissolved. America entered the war, and Hollywood was now able to use all the facilities at its disposal to help America win the war.

THE FILMS

There seemed to be no way that Warner, Zanuck, or Schenck could deny that Hollywood had been producing films encouraging American entry into the war since early 1939. Whether it was propaganda seemed questionable to the film moguls. As Zanuck claimed: "I usually find that when someone produces something that you do not like, they call it propaganda." Rather, they argued that they were presenting motion pictures which advocated a particular political position. They reasoned that others, given the rights of free speech, might produce films that supported isolationist ideas. In reality, however, no one did so.

The films which preceded American entry into the war were of two types: the metaphorical and the contemporary. The metaphorical films deliberately avoided the current European conflict. They often looked to history for valid analogies to the present political situation. These motion pictures argued that the American people should learn from the lessons of history that war was often necessary in order to defend democracy and the American way of life.

As a result the camera wandered through time and place to discover parallels of current events. For example, *Juarez* (1939) exalted a nineteenth century Mexican president, because he defended his nation against the dictatorial Napoleon III and supported democracy for Latin American nations. The rhetoric of the film bordered on the contemporary, causing Frank S. Nugent, critic for the *New York Times,* to note "that it is not at all difficult to read between the lines."

Perhaps the most popular film of this historical genre was an excursion into the American past with Howard Hawks' *Sergeant York.* Producers had attempted to film the life of this World War I hero since Jesse Lasky broached the idea in 1919. After years of negotiations, York finally allowed his biography to be filmed. Alvin York remained on the set during the entire filming, and later praised Warners for its historical accuracy.

Despite York's claims of the film's veracity, *Sergeant York* became yet another motion picture which advocated the

taking of arms in the defense of democracy. The young
Alvin York (Gary Cooper) finds religion after a misspent
youth. He reads the Bible diligently, and when drafted, refuses to fight, since he believes "Thou shall not kill." An
army major admires York's ability with a rifle but cannot
understand his reluctance to support the war. He gives
York a *History of the United States,* so the new recruit can
learn what the Founding Fathers and the great American
heroes once fought for. ("Daniel Boone wanted freedom.
That's quite a word, *freedom.*") York retreats to a mountain-
side to ponder the major's message. A wind blows the pages
of the Bible open to a quotation fraught with meaning:
"Render therefore to Caesar the things that are Caesar's,
and to God the things that are God's." A divine light shines
on York's face, and he realizes that he must fight to preserve
America's freedom. York has learned from history and
from the Bible that pacifism is irrelevant when the defense
of freedom is concerned. Warner Brothers hoped that the
audience would learn the same lesson.

The majority of films of this period avoided the indirect
approach and considered contemporary society. Some,
such as *Confessions of a Nazi Spy,* revealed Nazi activities on
the homefront. This factual account starred Edward G.
Robinson as the assiduous American agent who uncovered
a vast Nazi spy ring in the United States. The story itself
was lifted from trial records, as well as a series of the *New
York Post* articles written by Leon G. Turrou, a former
F.B.I. investigator.

Other films concerned German society and the rise of the
Nazi party. These films lacked the gritty reality of *Confessions of a Nazi Spy,* but attempted to fictionalize the horrors
of Hitler's Germany. *The Mortal Storm* (1941) is typical of
this genre. The family of Professor Roth (Frank Morgan)
is brutally destroyed as Nazi power is concentrated. Roth's
daughter, Freya, (Margaret Sullavan) defends the ideals of

freedom, while the male children actively support the Nazi cause. Professor Roth, an anatomist, is ousted from the university because he refuses to support theories of Aryan superiority. He is then arrested and sent to a concentration camp. Roth's family attempts to emigrate, but Freya is detained. She eventually attempts to flee through the Austrian mountains with her lover, a young idealist, portrayed by James Stewart, but she is shot by Nazi troops led by her former boyfriend (Robert Young).

Four Sons, I Married a Nazi, and *So Ends Our Night* also followed this pattern of the breaking of family ties in the face of the Nazi menace. Other films which considered Germany were primarily of the espionage type *(Man Hunt, Underground),* but they maintained a firm anti-Nazi position.

What remained a minor trend before American entry into the war, soon became a torrent after Pearl Harbor. No longer was there any attempt to limit films opposed to Nazi Germany or those praising American ideals. In the next four years, Hollywood produced countless films which attempted to win the war in the hearts and minds of American citizens.

HOLLYWOOD AT WAR

Life changed behind the screen as well. The active support of Washington's war policy was not only evident in the finished film product. Producers, directors, stars, extras, musicians, electricians, and carpenters gave more to the war effort than motion pictures. Hollywood's nightlife collapsed, and many restaurants remained open only on weekends. The carefree life of the previous decade dimmed considerably as the denizens of the film capital flocked to assist the war effort.

Volunteer organizations flourished shortly after Pearl Harbor. Stars joined every possible committee: the Volunteer Army Canteen Service, Bundles for Bluejackets, the Aerial Nurse Corps, the Women's Ambulance Defense Corps, and the Civil Air Patrol. They even became air raid spotters and wardens.

More than five hundred actors joined the Actors' Committee of the Hollywood Victory Committee for Stage, Screen, and Radio. This organization, headed by Clark Gable, arranged benefit performances for the Red Cross, Navy Relief Fund, and other wartime organizations. Others began cross-country tours to sell defense bonds. Carole Lombard was killed on one of these trips. Dorothy Lamour, known as the "Sweetheart of the Treasury," completed Lombard's itinerary and travelled more than ten thousand miles on visits to defense plants and shipyards.

Even film studios volunteered their services. The most noteworthy of these efforts was the contribution of half of the Walt Disney studios for films concerning defense projects. Donald Duck and Mickey Mouse thus appeared gratis in films for the Treasury Department and the Office of Inter-American Affairs.

General Lewis Hershey declared that the film industry was "essential" during wartime. As a result, he allowed studios to apply for draft deferments for irreplaceable workers. Despite the government's permission for major stars, directors, and writers to remain safely in Hollywood, many luminaries decided to enlist. Frank Capra, John Ford, Garson Kanin, William Wyler, and Darryl Zanuck offered their film-making talents to the War Department.

Actors also joined the exodus. Clark Gable departed soon after the death of his wife, Carole Lombard. James Stewart gained ten pounds so he could pass the physical and become a private. The numbers of leading men that deserted Hollywood during the war led to a crisis, as capable male actors became impossible to find for many new films.[4]

In this fashion, Hollywood became a major ally to Washington. While the film capital was seen as an antagonist in the days before Pearl Harbor, government advisors began to realize that the film industry could be of major help in the war effort. Leo Rosten, the novelist and a deputy director of the Office of War Information (OWI), explained the value of the motion picture to the American audience:

> The movies can give the public information. But they can do more than that; they can give the public understanding. They can clarify problems that are complex and confusing. They can focus attention upon the key problems which the people must decide, the basic choices which people make. They can make clear and intelligible the enormous complexities of global geography, military tactics, economic dilemmas, political disputes, and psychological warfare. The singularly illuminating tools of the screen can be used to give the people a clear, continuous, and comprehensible picture of the total pattern of total war.[5]

The motion picture seemed the ideal medium to fulfill OWI goals. Established in June 1942 by executive order, the OWI was designed to "disseminate war information" and facilitate the understanding of the "policies, activities, and aims of the Government" during World War II. Motion pictures could therefore play a vital role in this effort.

Despite Hollywood's willingness to help on a voluntary basis, it was no secret that the leaders of the film industry feared the imposition of government censorship. They were somewhat surprised when Lowell Mellett, head of the Bureau of Motion Pictures (BMP) of the OWI, explained to an audience of film producers that he was "hoping that most of you and your fellow workers would stay right here in Hollywood and keep on doing what you're doing, because your motion pictures are a vital contribution to the total defense effort." At first this statement bewildered the assembled film producers. When one asked Mellett if the industry should make "hate pictures," Mellett replied, "Use your own judgment. We'll give you our advice if you want us to."

Yet, the OWI was not going to sit passively on the sidelines. Mellett explained that his office would fulfill two functions. First, he would attempt to advise Hollywood about Washington's attitudes concerning future films. Producers could submit their ideas voluntarily to his office, which would then determine proper policy after discussion with the State Department. In this manner film plots concerning Russia or China, for example, would follow official foreign policy decisions. Despite Mellett's calming tone, the fine line between advice and censorship was often cloudy. Within a short time, Mellett's office would be perceived as the enemy as it began to insist that both scripts and dialogue be changed to suit the needs of the government.[6]

The BMP also coordinated Washington's entry into the film production game. Although the government had produced official films as early as 1900, wartime production reached new highs. The OWI could approve, reject, or request revisions in the multitude of government films designed for theatrical showing. Such motion pictures as *Tanks* (narrated by Orson Welles), *Bomber* (with commentary by Carl Sandburg), and *Army in Overalls* appeared in the nation's theatres. In the midst of these documentaries, a Donald Duck cartoon, *The New Spirit*, became one of the most popular films produced by the government.

Government policy affected not only what appeared on the screen, but also what occurred behind it. The War Production Board (WPB) issued a series of decrees in 1942, which were designed to control the profligate practices of the major studios, so that vital war materials might be conserved. The first ruling limited to $5,000 the amount that could be spent on sets for any one picture. The Board also suggested a sharp curtailment in film use. Budget analysts suggested the elimination of all filmed rehearsals and the use of single takes for rushes. One engineer even suggested that projection speeds be slowed from ninety to sixty-seven feet of film per minute. Although he claimed that more than 500 million feet of film would be saved each year, it would have meant that previously produced films could not be shown on these new projectors.

Hollywood took many of these suggestions to heart. When Frank S. Nugent visited the studios in 1942, he was stunned by the change:

> Say this for Hollywood: it rarely does things by halves. If it was magnificently extravagant a few years ago, it is being a magnificent miser today. Studio incinerators used to roar twenty-four hours a day. Lumber, doors, scaffolds, trim, paneling—enough for a real estate subdivision—were tossed to the furnaces. Nowadays, the lumber burned wouldn't build a respectable dollhouse. Sets are dismantled as carefully as time bombs: a carpenter who splits a board virtually is made to stand in the corner. . . . Hairpins— another vital product in a glamour creating town—are practically checked in and out of the dressing rooms, sterilized after each use.[7]

One studio even tried to invent a nail straightening machine in order to recycle no. 8 nails which were in great demand by the wartime industries.

Thus, both before and behind the screen, Hollywood life was greatly affected by the coming of war. The massive changes in American society pervaded the industry, coloring the films produced during this era both consciously and unconsciously. Even the musical comedy was not immune.

PART TWO

THE EVOLUTION
OF THE
HOLLYWOOD MUSICAL

2

The Musical
of the Great Depression

The musical film at first seems an unlikely candidate for the acceptance of wartime responsibilities. Often considered the most escapist of film genres, the musical has gained notoriety for its devil-may-care attitude toward the contemporary world. Yet, this reputation is not entirely deserved. From the early days of sound, the Hollywood musical has paid a healthy respect to the real world in its form if not in its content.

Mervyn LeRoy noticed this paradox during the filming of *The Wizard of Oz* (1939), as studio executives repeatedly tried to cut "Over the Rainbow" from the final print of the film. They argued that there was no reason for a young girl to sing a wistful ballad in the middle of a Kansas barnyard. No one complained about the evil witches, a talking lion, flying monkeys, a tin woodsman, or a dancing scarecrow. In the Land of Oz anything could happen as all logic was suspended in that world of fantasy. However, no one sings in a Kansas barnyard.[1]

LeRoy's firm insistence on the matter eventually convinced M-G-M advisors to allow Judy Garland to sing the

Harold Arlen and E. Y. Harburg ballad, and the song soon became a classic. This anecdote is revealing of the rigid bonds of logic that governed the Hollywood musical comedy for many years. Despite talk of "fantasy" and "escapism" whenever the musical genre is discussed, film musicals were inextricably bound to the real world.

This inconsistency disturbed Lorenz Hart when he and the young Richard Rodgers left Broadway for Hollywood in the early 1930s. Again studio executives expected the talented songwriting team to produce works similar to those they had written for Broadway. However, when Hart attempted to insert rhythmic dialogue in such films as *Hot Heiress* (1931) and *Love Me Tonight* (1932), producers kept asking him why people were unexpectedly breaking into song. "How can you do this?" they asked. "Where's the cue?"[2]

The authors of Broadway musicals at this time faced a different set of assumptions from writers of film musicals. Song was expected in Broadway musicals of the late 1920s and early 1930s, and all denizens of the stage show might participate in the merriment no matter their identity. For example, politicians could sing of presidential elections in *Of Thee I Sing* (1931); the blacks of Catfish Row in *Porgy and Bess* (1935) might express their innermost feelings in song; and even Public Enemy Number One could recite the virtues of crime in lyric form in *Anything Goes* (1934). These occurrences were not jarring to the Broadway audience; on the contrary, the immediate and unexplained recourse to song was expected. George Abbott, noted director of several Broadway musicals, once commented, "Give me a great song and with two lines of dialogue I can slip it into any show." The modern goal of integration of song and libretto did not flower until the mid-1940s.

In Hollywood, however, the reverse became true. The coming of sound to the hitherto silent world of the feature film heralded a new fidelity to the real world. The addition of dialogue would allow the motion picture camera to reproduce the reality of daily life with unparalleled accuracy, as both sound and image became one.

The Hollywood musical comedy was born with the birth of sound, and from that date it experienced logical restrictions that its Broadway parent never had to endure. Although not the first feature film to integrate song into its plot, *The Jazz Singer* (1927) was billed as the first all-singing, all-talking motion picture.[3] This Warner Brothers-First National production featured Al Jolson as Jackie, a cantor's son, who becomes a world-wide celebrity. When the cantor discovers that his son would rather sing in a nightclub than in the synagogue, he disowns him. Years later, the errant Jackie returns to New York to assume the lead in a Broadway show. The elderly cantor falls ill on the show's opening night, which also happens to be the most important Jewish Holy Day, Yom Kippur. Jackie is tormented by this event, but he ultimately decides to sing the Kol Nidre at the synagogue in order to please his father. The cantor hears his son's voice through an open window, and he smiles and dies happily.

The musical numbers in *The Jazz Singer* were naturally tailored for Jolson. He mugs, cavorts, and twists in whiteface and black. But he is always performing, and he is always on stage. Thus, there is always a logical reason for Jolson's singing. He is little Jackie singing for pennies, the star on the Broadway stage, or the substitute cantor in the synagogue. He never breaks into song without motivation. This was no constraint for Jolson, since he performed as he did in nightclubs or on Broadway. However, it represented the constraints that prevented the film musical from developing beyond its initial logical assumptions, namely, that all song and dance must be limited to a performance situation.

Ironically, the musicals of the 1930s are often remembered for the mad excesses of Busby Berkeley or the elegance of Fred Astaire and Ginger Rogers. Despite the carefree memories of this era, the musical seemed even more locked into the conventions that Jolson and company had initiated.

Busby Berkeley rarely directed his own musical films in the thirties. More often than not Lloyd Bacon or Mervyn LeRoy directed the "plot" sequences of the film, while Berkeley choreographed the show-stopping finale, usually a sequence of dance numbers. These two parts of the film differed considerably. The narrative segment provided the explanation for the later musical scenes. The usual excuse for the extravagant dance numbers was that Dick Powell was composing songs for a new musical or James Cagney was producing a new stage show. The same characters inhabited most of the Warners' musicals—chorines, composers, lyricists, tap-dancers, pianists, writers, producers and choreographers. All of these show business folk had a logical reason to participate in the song and dance numbers as rehearsals, backers' auditions, and out-of-town tryouts provided the rationale for the musical numbers.

The plot sequences of these Warners' films proved secondary to the Busby Berkeley production numbers. Despite the fond remembrances of the Berkeley extravagance, it must be remembered that he, too, was constrained by the concept of the "show," whether a charity performance in *Gold Diggers of 1935*, a series of musical shorts in *Footlight Parade*, or a Broadway show in *Gold Diggers of 1933* and *Dames*.

The Berkeley numbers habitually appeared in the last reel of the film. An audience is present, poised, and quiet. The camera pans the waiting audience. Cut to the stage. The curtain rises, and the rules which limited the writers in earlier segments of the film suddenly disappear. Even the stage itself seemingly vanishes and becomes a space the size of three Grand Central Stations or several Olympic swimming pools.

The Berkeley stage demonstrates a nodding acceptance of the rules governing the musical. But once the perfunctory curtain is raised, all pretenses of reality disappear. This stage resembles no Broadway prototype, as space and scenes dissolve at a speed no Shubert Alley stagehand could ever hope to duplicate. While the actors of the first segment of the film are once again reunited in this supposed performance, they are no longer bound by the limits of logic. Ruby Keeler may divide into hundreds of identical twins in *Dames*, Al Jolson may fly through the heavens in *Wonderbar* (1934), and animated underwear may dance with Joan Blondell in *Dames*.

The construction of Berkeley's dance numbers is not bound by the logic and reality of everyday life. More often than not, Berkeley's classic dance numbers resemble a game of free association, as the film progresses by repetitive images rather than by an orderly plot. For example, in the "Lullaby of Broadway" number from *Gold Diggers of 1935*, the audience sees a working girl sharpening a pencil. Suddenly, as the workday ends, Berkeley shifts to the image of the organ grinder, cranking his machine in the same rhythmic motion as the girl at the pencil sharpener.

Similarly, the song lyrics might suggest an idea to Berkeley. In Harry Warren and Al Dubin's "I Only Have Eyes for You" *(Dames)*, Dick Powell sings "All others disappear from view" whenever he sees Ruby Keeler's face. Suddenly, all the people on a busy Manhattan street also "disappear from view" as if by magic. Likewise, the lyric continues, mentioning that "others join in song," and previously indifferent passersby begin to sing with him.

Yet, there is a sense of discomfort in these extravagant dance sequences, as though the dance director is hindered by the knowledge that he must return to the reality of the stage on which the number began. Thus, despite these excesses, Berkeley always realized that he must say goodbye to the displays of dancing pianos or marble swimming pools and return his performers to center stage of the pre-Broadway tryout.

Berkeley's standard method of return is the reversal of the direction of the dance number, retracing the illogical steps that initially brought him to the fantastic configurations of his greatest scenes. For example, the "Lullaby of Broadway" number ends as it began. The fun-loving playgirl accidentally falls to her death from the window of a celestial nightclub at the climax of the scene. Yet, the dance does not end at this point. The scene returns to the images of the woman's apartment, and her lonely cat waiting for its milk. The skyline of New York City reappears, and the silhouette slowly transforms into the face of Winifred Shaw, alone on a dark stage. The face then floats in mid-air, and gradually progresses backstage, disappearing from the view of the audience. This sequence reverses the opening scenes of this number and allows Berkeley to return the cast to center stage. The curtain falls, and the audience applauds.

Thus, the screen audience is never allowed to forget that it is watching a stage show, in which song, as a substitute for dialogue, is perfectly acceptable. All the love songs that present-day audiences remember from the musicals of the 1930s were mainly stage production numbers, such as "I Only Have Eyes for You." Despite the romantic nature of such songs, the duet was the exception rather than the rule, as an ensemble of performers were responsible for etching these songs in one's memory.

The nine Fred Astaire and Ginger Rogers films at RKO during this period would at first seem to be an exception to this trend, as duets in song and dance predominated in these motion pictures. Similarly, no one could repress Fred Astaire, as almost without notice, in living rooms, bedrooms, or city streets, he would inexplicably break into song and dance, and, if Ginger were present, she would join him.

Yet, despite this freedom to break into song and dance, the Astaire and Rogers films were always hindered by excessive plot devices that attempted to rationalize such acts. Fred was invariably cast as a dancer or a bandleader in these films. Such a device appeared necessary to explain Astaire's love for music and his penchant for dancing at the most inopportune moments. Interestingly, while Astaire was cast as a talented hoofer in the film version of *The Gay Divorcee*, the stage versions in both New York and London featured him as a noted novelist. On stage, no complicated plot device was found necessary to explain Astaire's continual dancing. Of all the RKO films, only in one, *Carefree* (1938), did Astaire not portray a musician or a dancer. Here he played Tony Flagg, psychiatrist. But even then he had to rationalize his choreographic expertise by announcing to Ginger: "I always wanted to be a dancer. Psychiatry showed me I was wrong."

Ginger was never hampered by the same constraints. While part of the time she appears as a dance instructress *(Swing Time)*, a professional entertainer *(Carefree)*, or a former vaudeville partner of Astaire *(Follow the Fleet)*, she is also presented in other films as a wealthy woman who, surprisingly, possesses a unique ability to follow the master's lead in dance and song.

Once these conventions were established, the writers, composers, and lyricists of the Astaire-Rogers films faced the dilemma of integrating these now classic dance routines into the musical. Mark Sandrich, who directed five of these films, reputedly hated unmotivated dance numbers and avoided them like the plague. By way of comparison, consider two of Fred and Ginger's classic routines, "The Carioca" and "The Continental," just one year apart. In *Flying Down to Rio* (1933), directed by Thornton Freeland, Fred and Ginger portray a band musician and a vocalist on tour in Brazil. Fred lures the band leader to the Carioca Casino to hear the native rhythms, which are proving considerably more popular than the North American melodies. The band members are both surprised and appalled by the sensuous nature of the Latin dance, the "Carioca." Fred and Ginger watch for a few minutes in a state of shock until Ginger snaps: "We'll show them a thing or three," and they take to the dance floor.

This reveals a marked contrast with "The Continental" number from *The Gay Divorcee*, directed by Sandrich in 1934. No longer do Fred and Ginger view the latest dance craze and immediately join the natives and outshine them at their own game. Here, Ginger portrays a potential divorcee, about to be trapped with a corespondent in a seaside hotel, so she can rid herself of her unwanted husband. Fred complicates the situation by pursuing Ginger to her hotel room. The gigolo prevents Fred and Ginger from leaving lest they sabotage his scheme. As a result, they hide in the bedroom, where, hearing the music from the hotel night club, they pretend to dance. In reality, however, they perch two cut-out paper dolls atop the revolving turntable of the record player. Fred shines a bright light on the tiny dancing images, and their six-foot revolving shadows present the illusion of a dancing couple, thus fooling the gigolo. Only then are Fred and Ginger free to escape from the apartment and begin "The Continental." Thus, even in the carefree Astaire and Rogers musicals, plot considerations and the importance of logic came to overpower the potential freedom of the musical genre.[4]

Ironically, these musicals which adhered to the basic realities of everyday life became the most popular and most remembered films of the 1930s, while those that attempted to expand or deny logical expectations were often dismal failures. These less successful, but often more ambitious, films hearkened back to the fantastic musical world created by the Frenchman René Clair. Clair's musical films were never populated with the backstage performers so common to Hollywood films. Clair's world presented common folk, bums, tailors, streetsingers, bartenders, and working men and women, and allowed them all to be capable of song. The open nature of this assumption is revealed by the fact that Clair even permitted the nonhuman beings, such as flowers and animals, to join in song in *A Nous La Liberté*. In Clair's films, music and song are accepted features of reality. There is no surprise if anyone (or anything) breaks into song. In this manner, Clair expanded the musical comedy tradition that had been inherited from Broadway and suggested that the musical film, a hybrid form, might break all the limitations that the static Broadway stage had imposed. The camera might accomplish scene changes in a fraction of a second, and as a result, the musical film need not be rooted in the linear and chronological progression of the Broadway musical.

Few Hollywood musicals of this era recognized this potential. Lorenz Hart argued that "the ideal musical comedy of the pictures would kill the musical comedy of the stage." He had no fears that he would lose his main source of livelihood, thanks to the parochial vision of film executives. He criticized the irony that "studios take stage writers to write stage stuff for the screen." He tried to counter this expectation, but producers thought he and Richard Rodgers were "blotto."

Hart attempted to pioneer a new form of film musical, but his efforts were continually frustrated. While other musical comedy writers, such as Irving Berlin, devoted most of their attention to the story conferences when they arrived in Hollywood, Hart was consistently on the set and sticking his nose into all aspects of feature production. He was most fascinated by the editing process, and, as a result, believed that musicals "should be written for the camera," and not be mere duplications of Broadway stage successes.

One of Rodgers and Hart's best film collaborations, *Love Me Tonight*, directed by Rouben Mamoulian, reveals this new relationship of music and song to the progression of the film. Maurice Chevalier, a tailor, sings "Isn't It Romantic?" in his tiny shop. A customer picks up the melody and sings quietly as he leaves the shop and enters a taxi. The cab driver hears the tune, and, he, too, begins singing. The song thus travels through the city as different people are captivated by the clever melody. Eventually, a troop of soldiers latch on to the melody, convert it to a marching rhythm, and carry it throughout the countryside. Finally, Jeanette MacDonald, at her distant castle, hears the song and begins to sing. In this instance, the song has emerged as an editing device, allowing Jeanette MacDonald to be introduced to the audience and her relationship to the tailor established. The music is thus used to carry the film forward, and all necessity of dialogue is eliminated.

Rodgers and Hart also attempted to pioneer yet another musical form—rhythmic dialogue—in their first Hollywood films.[5] This less successful effort was based on the assumption that there should be no clear divisions between the dialogue and musical portions of the film. As a result, a rhythmic musical dialogue, almost a patter-song, emerged. At times the rhythm for the dialogue would be established by a dominant thematic sound, as in *Hot Heiress*, where the noise of the riveter's drill press supplied the pace and tempo for the film's opening dialogue. At other times, as in *Fools for Scandal* (1938) or *Love Me Tonight*, this rhythmic patter would begin unexpectedly and end just as suddenly. The themes of this rhythmic, but not always rhym-

ing, dialogue were often commonplace. The following example from *Love Me Tonight* illustrates the pacing and brev-
ity of this format. The doctor states to Jeanette MacDonald:

DOCTOR:	Now, my dear, remove your dress.
JEANETTE:	My what?
DOCTOR:	Your dress. There's no occasion for distress.
JEANETTE:	Is it necessary?
DOCTOR:	Very . . . yes . . . as long as professional eth-ics apply, I'll see you with a doctor's eye.

Rodgers and Hart had only one brief opportunity to expand the concept of rhythmic dialogue to an entire film,
Hallelujah, I'm a Bum (1933), directed by Lewis Milestone.
Audiences seemed to reject this new style of musical film,
and its failure helped to sour Rodgers and Hart on Hollywood. When they returned to film musicals in the 1940s,
they abandoned the concept of rhythmic dialogue and duplicated the stage conventions of Broadway shows in such
films as *Too Many Girls* and *They Met in Argentina*. *Hallelujah,
I'm a Bum* failed at the box office for yet another reason.
It was one of the few musicals to tackle the Great Depression as its main theme. The film was populated by a contin-
gent of tramps who roamed the streets of New York City.
Some, such as Harry Langdon, even voiced thoughts of social revolution.

While the majority of film musicals of the 1930s accepted
the real world in terms of form, they generally ignored it
in terms of content. With the exception of *Hallelujah, I'm
a Bum*, few films utilized the Depression as a plot device.
Only rarely did the economic crisis intrude on the generally blissful musical world of the early 1930s.

Gold Diggers of 1933 is perhaps the most famous exception. As the film opens, Ginger Rogers steps forward and
sings "We're in the Money" before a backdrop of twenty-
foot-high silver coins. Even her dress is a collection of nick-

els and dimes sewn on a silvery fabric. As Ginger sings the song in "pig Latin" ("Ere-way in-ay the oney-may"), the sheriff appears and seizes the sets and costumes because the producer was unable to pay the bills. Before the glittering scenery, the stark reality of the Depression becomes readily apparent.

The showgirls' ultimate solution for their sudden unemployment is to marry millionaires, a remedy of little worth to the viewing audience. The sugar daddies supply funds for a new show, and, as a demonstration that the company has not forgotten the horrors of poverty, Joan Blondell sings "Remember the Forgotten Man," a moving tribute to the Bonus Marchers of 1932.

Gold Diggers of 1933 was one of the few films to acknowledge the serious state of the American economy. This led to a curious schizophrenia in the majority of musical films. While the form of the musical of the 1930s was dependent on the logic of the real world, in matters of content it was not. As a result, the musical film remained curiously divorced from the tensions affecting American society during this traumatic period. This sense of alienation, however, was not to last for long. As the coming of World War II boosted the flagging American economy, the mobilization for war also revived the musical film, giving it a definitive commitment to the problems of the society it had previously ignored.

3

Prelude to War (1937-1941)

By 1937 the Hollywood musical was in a state of crisis. Musical films were not drawing audiences as they had during the early years of the Depression. Warner Brothers began to dismantle its music department and abruptly fired Harry Warren, composer of the Gold Diggers extravaganzas, because it would be cheaper to hire composers and lyricists for individual films.[1]

A year later musicals dwindled to a mere fraction of previous output. M-G-M announced that only one out of six future films would be musicals, while Columbia scheduled none in its list of future productions. Although Warner Brothers did plan a film version of the 1939 Broadway musical *On Your Toes,* the completed motion picture eliminated most of the classic Rodgers and Hart songs.[2]

The abrupt decline in the production of musical films caused a major employment crisis in the West Coast studios, as the foremost contributors to the Hollywood musical returned to Shubert Alley. *Variety* noted a massive migration as "tunesmiths, librettists, stagers, dance directors, and others converged back on Broadway as their chief outlet of creative expression." Hollywood's loss was Broadway's gain. The casting director for a proposed Jerome

31

Kern and Oscar Hammerstein musical claimed that he expected to cast fifty percent of his show from Hollywood exiles. "New York," he explained, "hasn't enough available talent."[3]

While Irving Berlin, Cole Porter, Hammerstein, and Kern were able to return to their native Broadway, other participants in Hollywood musicals were not in such an enviable position. The rising numbers of unemployed dancers caused a panic at central casting. Many former chorus members changed their listing to "dress extra." The pay was lower, but at least the extras were being hired.[4]

The disappearance of the chorus marked a major departure for the film musical of the late thirties. *The New York Times* noted this trend almost immediately: "*Gold Diggers in Paris* (1938) showed an amazingly restrained Busby Berkeley. *Goldwyn Follies* (1938) did not have a large ensemble. *Artists and Models Abroad* (1938) will use no big production numbers. *Carefree* (1938) used only dress extras on its biggest sets." The new musicals were "intimate," which was often a euphemism for inexpensive. Any musical film costing more than $600,000 could not hope to make a profit in the tuneless atmosphere of the late Depression years. When Warner Brothers dropped Dick Powell's option, the only large scale musicals being produced featured performers in which the studios had major contractual investments. As a result, Jeanette MacDonald and Nelson Eddy (M-G-M) and Bing Crosby (Paramount) bridged these years of musical retrenchment.[5]

Smallness is not necessarily a saleable commodity. For audiences that had been trained to welcome massive chorus numbers, something had to be offered in exchange. Darryl F. Zanuck claimed that he discovered the key to the new Hollywood musical. He argued that the "modern" musical should have a "timely or news interest." He explained in a *New York Times* interview that:

Thanks A Million (1935) dealt in a humorous way with politics as the presidential campaign was getting under way; *Sing, Baby, Sing* (1936) whirled about a Caliban-Ariel situation that had a counterpart on the front page. *Pigskin Parade* (1936) appeared as the football season was getting hot. *Wake Up and Live* (1937), with Walter Winchell and Ben Bernie, appeared at a time when a radio comedian wasn't a radio comedian unless he was insulting another radio comedian.[6]

With this emphasis on the topical, Zanuck managed to prune the musical down to size. He cut the elaborate chorus numbers, which had formerly delighted audiences, and substituted contemporary humor. The largest chorus number in a Zanuck produced musical of this period appeared in Irving Berlin's *On the Avenue* (1937), which featured twenty-four dancers in a single sequence. *Pigskin Parade* had only one ensemble number, and *Sing, Baby, Sing* had none at all.

These films marked quite a change from the Busby Berkeley successes of the early 1930s. And where was Berkeley during this transition period? Warners let his option drop after he directed *They Made Me a Criminal* (1939), a crime drama with John Garfield. He drifted to M-G-M, but was kept in tight rein for the interim. His classic style remained expensive and out of favor with studio heads.

The result was a short, snappy, streamlined musical from Twentieth Century-Fox. Inexpensive to produce, these new films introduced a new dimension to the Hollywood musical: topicality. In the early thirties, the musical had generally avoided the stark reality of the Depression and created a mythical world. By 1939, current events had become fair game for the musical film. At first, the notion of contemporaneity included references to politics, sports, and the film industry. As echoes of war began to be heard throughout the world, Hollywood was able to present the dominant issue of the day in musical format. A subject that had formerly been taboo for an "escapist" genre began to shape the form and content of the new musical comedies.

The most noticeable response to the European conflict was the advent of a patriotic musical which stressed the importance of the American value system. *Let Freedom Ring* (M-G-M 1939) directed by Jack Conway, was an early example of this genre. *Variety* noted that this film was "the first in a cycle of film offerings to stress American type democracy and freedom for the classes and masses."[7]

In many ways *Let Freedom Ring* was similar to other nonmusical films of the era. Like *Sergeant York* and *Juarez,* the Nelson Eddy and Virginia Bruce musical avoided direct mention of the European conflict by the use of historical metaphor. *Let Freedom Ring* utilized the Wild West of the nineteenth century in order to prove that ethnic and religious tolerance could be accomplished by peaceful means rather than by warfare.

The Ben Hecht screenplay analyzed the struggles between the western landowners and the forces of "progress," as represented by the corrupt railroad owner, Jim Knox (Edward Arnold). Knox owns everything in the small town of Clover City including Judge Bronson (Guy Kibbee), who facilitates Knox's plan to buy cheap land for his railroad.

When Steve Logan (Nelson Eddy) returns to his hometown, everyone hopes that he will set the situation right. Much to the townfolk's horror, Steve has become an alcoholic. He then allies with Knox and becomes his private troubadour. The town looks on Steve's actions with disgust, but they do not realize that it is merely an act. He is actually a government agent who wishes to discover evidence that will convict Knox.

Steve tries to convince the immigrant railroad workers of Knox's illegal activities by stealing the town's printing press and publishing an underground newspaper. ("If we could only get the truth to them, we might turn them into Americans.") The newspaper urges the workers to vote for Steve's father, Tom Logan (Lionel Barrymore), for judge. If the workers vote in this fashion, Knox can be convicted for his land speculation schemes.

Knox discovers Steve's true identity and attempts to have him killed. This fails and Knox's men set Tom's barn ablaze. "What is it?" "It's America burning," answers Steve. Nothing will stop Knox, and he tries to hang both of the Logans. Steve makes an impassioned speech to the railway workers concerning the importance of freedom, while his girl friend, Maggie (Virginia Bruce), begins to sing "America." Steve's words and Maggie's song win over the town. The crowd deserts Knox, and opts for freedom to the strains of "America."[8]

Let Freedom Ring denounced mob violence, dictatorship, and tyranny, while it praised the great American melting pot. The message was hardly hidden in the Wild West atmosphere. Indeed, Frank S. Nugent jokingly commented in the *New York Times* that he "didn't dare criticize it adversely under penalty of being summoned before the Dies committee," which was then investigating Communist activity in Hollywood.

Most of the musicals in the period before American entry into the war did not assume the patriotic stance of *Let Freedom Ring*. Nevertheless, the coming of war seemed to threaten the jovial world of the musical comedy. Despite the economic catastrophe of the 1930s, spirits remained high in the musicals of the early Depression years. Although backers might not be found for a new show, as in *Gold Diggers of 1933*, the performers rarely lost their sense of humor or feeling of hope. Events inevitably justified this optimism as funds for the show were always found during the last moments of the film. Tempers rarely flared, and everything was resolved peacefully.

The atmosphere changed abruptly as the threat of war heightened. The tone of the new musical became bitter and confused. Many musicals of the transition period of 1939 to 1941 may not have discussed the coming of war, but it is certain that tensions of the era began to affect them. What happened to the backstage composers, lyricists, and performers who populated the early film musicals in the period before Pearl Harbor?

Warner Brothers' *Naughty But Nice* (1939) was the last of the old-fashioned backstage musicals. It was also the last performance of the studio's veteran Dick Powell before his contract was terminated. Thus, this film symbolized the end of an era rather than the beginning of a new age. The tone of this film is relentlessly comic. Professor Donald Hardwick (Powell), a music professor at staid Winfield College, is vehemently opposed to the latest trends in music. Linda McKay (Ann Sheridan), a popular song lyricist, sets words to Hardwick's latest classic rhapsody. His tone poem is converted to "Hooray for Spinach," which immediately hits the top of the charts. Hardwick first resists the switch to popular music, but he is won over by the lovely Linda and the antics of the comic song pushers Allan Jenkins, Jerry Colonna, and Slapsie Maxie Rosenbloom. Composer and lyricist marry, and all is resolved happily for the most popular songwriting team in the country.

By 1941, however, the mythical world of the backstage musical seemed dead as bitterness, jealousy, and even murder came to the fore. The tranquil and jovial atmosphere of the 1930s is shattered by such new backstage musicals as *Lady Be Good* and *Blues in the Night*.

From its opening moments, *Lady Be Good* (1941) reverses the standard boy-meets-girl formula. Here Dixie Crane (Ann Sothern) stands in the Court of Domestic Relations before Judge Lionel Barrymore and requests a divorce from her husband, Eddie (Robert Young). She explains to the judge in a lengthy flashback why their marriage soured. At first all is blissful as the Cranes begin to write songs together. They compose the hit "You'll Never Know," and a successful songwriting team is born.

Soon the marriage begins to dissolve. Dixie's friend Marilyn (Eleanor Powell) testifies to the court that the "marriage was a flop." Why? "Eddie went Park Avenue." Eddie flits from party to party as Dixie becomes alienated from his society friends. She decides that Eddie would be happier if he were alone.

Barrymore grants the divorce. Eddie's personal life swiftly becomes a mess. Dixie's problems are professional; it becomes more difficult to write new lyrics. Eddie resolves to return and help Dixie with her songwriting. They swiftly write a successful tune. Satisfied with their day's efforts, they retreat to the bedroom. Suddenly, Dixie recalls that she and Eddie are no longer married, and she chases him from the apartment.

Eddie's anger and jealousy grow as he discovers that Buddy Crawford (John Carroll) has started to date Dixie. Eddie tries to punch Buddy at a local restaurant, but Buddy dodges and clobbers him. Eddie holds his blackened eye and shouts: "You'll never sing one of my songs on the air." He then returns to his club for several stiff drinks.

Eddie tries to be nice to Dixie by showering her with flowers. She agrees to meet him and in one afternoon they compose the number-one song hit "Lady Be Good" with nary a nod to George and Ira Gershwin, the song's real composers. When the song tops the charts, Dixie and Eddie are invited to a banquet held in their honor by the profession's most popular songwriters.

It is only at this point that the image of the war intrudes. Dixie is invited to sing her new song hit "The Last Time I Saw Paris." Max, the toastmaster, explains the urgency of the song to the audience:

They've given the world another great song. When you hear Dixie sing it, I think you'll feel as I do that this isn't just another work by two songwriters. It's as if they had 100,000,000 collaborators—the Americans who feel in their hearts what Eddie and Dixie have written so beautifully in their song. I refer to the tender and affectionate salute to a lost city—"The Last Time I Saw Paris."

In this fashion the reality of a world at war invades a musical that had previously concerned itself only with domestic discord. Dixie strides to the platform and begins to sing:

The last time I saw Paris
Her heart was warm and gay
No matter how they change her
I'll remember her that way.*

As she sings, images of Paris, the sidewalk cafes, the Champs Élysées, the Eiffel Tower, and the Arc de Triomphe are superimposed on her face.

Although Eddie and Dixie claim credit for this inspiring song, it was actually written by Jerome Kern and Oscar Hammerstein II. Hammerstein also authored Max's introduction to the song in *Lady Be Good,* and, as might be expected, Max expressed Hammerstein's feelings when he wrote the song in 1940. At that time Paris had fallen, and Hammerstein was supposed to be working on a new musical, *Sunny River,* with Sigmund Romberg. However, Hammerstein was unable to work since visions of his recent trip to Paris continually flashed before his eyes. He telephoned Jerome Kern and read him the lyric for his new song, and Kern completed the music within one week. This was the first time in their on-again, off-again collaboration that

Hammerstein had written the lyrics *before* Kern had finished the music. Arthur Freed purchased the song for *Lady Be Good* and insisted that Hammerstein prepare the introduction.[9] Fortunately, the true authors were honored when "The Last Time I Saw Paris" won the 1941 Academy Award for "Best Song."

As Dixie returns to her seat, the images of the lost city begin to fade. After the dinner Eddie asks Dixie to marry him again. She refuses since she believes that they can write better songs if they remain divorced. Eddie then resolves never to see her again.

But Eddie's jealousy cannot be controlled. He threatens to shoot Buddy Crawford, and his display of anger proves to Dixie that Eddie really loves her. They drive to the country and remarry. As they return, Eddie explains that they will spend their honeymoon at a mansion belonging to his society friends. "No," says Dixie, "work first, vacation second." She decides to live with Marilyn until they finish the score for their new Broadway show. Eddie will not live alone, so he kicks her out of the car, and Dixie is forced to hitch a ride back to New York. Dixie works on the show herself, and Eddie decides to write a symphony.

Dixie returns to Barrymore's court. He, however, denies the second divorce and admonishes Dixie to "go home and behave" herself. Eddie regrets his actions and rushes to meet Dixie outside the courtroom: "From now on it's only you. I want you to marry me again." They embrace as the film ends, and the entire cast sings "Lady Be Good."

Is this a musical or *Divorce Court?* This is certainly a far cry from *Naughty, But Nice* and the backstage musicals of the 1930s. *Lady Be Good* was not alone in this dark vision of married life. Two other 1941 films *(Orchestra Wives* and *Ziegfeld Girl)* added alcoholism, wife abuse, infidelity, and neurosis to their musical sagas of marital discord. Yet, these films seemed a delight when compared to another 1941 tale of backstage life, *Blues in the Night,* which plunged the musical into new depths of despair.

Blues in the Night, named after the Harold Arlen-Johnny Mercer song, ventured further backstage than any other musical had dared. This Anatole Litvak film begins with the formation of a band which specializes in "blues, the sound of the people." The new band is hardly famous, as they are forced to travel from gig to gig in a railroad boxcar. On one of their jaunts, an escaped criminal (Lloyd Nolan) joins the band in the boxcar. He is the owner of the "Jungle" nightclub, which has yet to turn a profit. He offers the band a stint at the club, which, to the group's surprise, turns out to be a gambling casino.

As soon as the band arrives at the "Jungle," tension begins to build. Band member Leo (Jack Carson) immediately falls in love with the gangster's moll, Kay Grant (Betty Field). The group is upset by this development, especially Leo's wife (Priscilla Lane), the band's lead singer. The moll is resented by everyone since she is "busting up the unit." Leo finally discovers that his wife is pregnant. He realizes the error of his ways, drops the moll, and rejoins the band at rehearsals. Kay leaves, and the unity is restored. When the baby is born, all members of the band respond to the new infant as if he were their own child. At last happiness returns to the band.

Yet, Kay the troublemaker returns once more. This time her goal is Jigger (Richard Whorf). He is so enraptured by Kay that he urges his fellow musicians to allow her to join the band. They resist because Kay cannot sing a note. Jigger is infuriated by the decision and strikes out on his own. He continues to play, but it is "smooth stuff and without feeling."

Jigger is haunted by his decision to leave the band. In a glittering montage sequence, filmed by Don Siegel, Jigger dreams of the band he has deserted. He envisions a huge hand with each member of the band as a finger. Jigger has broken the unity of the band and has destroyed the hand. This delirium drives him to a nervous breakdown. He and Kay split up during this time of trouble. But the band members never forget a friend in need. They return to Jigger, remind him of the importance of the blues, and urge him to play with the group once again.

Naturally, Kay returns after Jigger recovers and once again begins to cause trouble. This time she murders her gangster friend. However, she has transgressed the musical moral code once too often. Brad (Wallace Ford), the Club's cripple-in-residence, kills Kay in a car "accident." The villains are thus eliminated in the last few moments of the film and order is restored. The band returns to riding the rails, and they sing "Hang On to Your Lids, Kids, Here We Go Again," as the film ends:

Ben Franklin once said it all
Divided we gotta fall.
United we'll have a ball.
Hang on to your lids kids,
Here we go again.*

Blues in the Night clearly demonstrated a preoccupation that dominated the Warners' musical during World War II—the importance of unity. The hand image of Jigger's dream symbolizes this ideal. Human society is like a hand. If the latter loses a finger or thumb, the function of the whole is impaired. However, if the fingers and thumb work together, the hand can function as a finely-tuned instrument. If Americans work together in this fashion, World War II can be won easily. If disunity prevails, however, all will be lost. This became the basic moral lesson of the Warners' musical at war.

---

*"Hang On to Your Lids, Kids, Here We Go Again." © 1941 Warner Bros., Inc. Copyright renewed. All rights reserved. Used by permission.

4

The Warner Brothers Musical at War

During the 1930s Warner Brothers became known as the studio with a social conscience. With such films as *I Am a Fugitive from a Chain Gang* (1932), *Black Legion* (1937), and *Wild Boys of the Road* (1933), Warners grabbed film plots from the headlines of the daily papers. When current events shifted to the widening European war in 1939 and 1940, it came as no surprise that Warner Brothers was among the first studios to dramatize this event on film. The shift in emphasis revealed more than a desire for a quick profit from these war-themed efforts. Both Jack and Harry Warner claimed it was their duty to expose the growing threat of Hitler and the Nazi party to the citizens of the United States.

Jack Warner violently opposed Hitler, Naziism, and anti-Semitism. He recalled the murder of his friend Joe Kauffman, a Warners' representative in Germany, who was beaten to death in an alley by Nazi agents, and vowed to resist Hitler's activities as best he could. He believed that film could play a vital role in the struggle with the Axis powers. One afternoon, Warner claimed, Bugsy Siegel visited his office and offered to liquidate Goebbels and Goering for him. Warner calmed the excitable gangster by explaining that he was "planning to make a picture called *Confessions of a Nazi Spy* which would hurt Herr Goebbels more than Bugsy Siegel's chopper."

Other producers urged him not to make the film, since they feared the loss of German film revenues. Warner replied, "Listen, these murdering bastards killed our own man in Germany because he wouldn't heil Hitler. The silver shirts and the Bundists are marching in Los Angeles right now. Is that what you want in exchange for some crummy film royalties from Germany? I'm going to finish this picture and Hitler and Goebbels can scream all they want."[1] Harry Warner, then president of the studio, strongly agreed with his brother and insisted that the film be made.

With such films as *Confessions of a Nazi Spy, Sergeant York*, and *Juarez*, Warners demonstrated the importance of democratic principles and the insidious nature of the Nazi menace in its dramatic films. It was only a matter of time before the musical comedy would voice the same message. Yet, the musical did not heed the war cry as swiftly as Warners' dramatic efforts. By the end of the 1930s, Warner Brothers had almost ceased production of musical films due to rising expenses and diminishing profits for this type of film. The company allowed Harry Warren, Busby Berkeley, and Dick Powell to leave for other studios when their contracts expired in 1939. As a result, musicals at Warners were in a state of disarray. In 1940 Warner Brothers produced no musicals for the first time since the birth of sound motion pictures.

The two new musicals produced in 1941 symbolized the amorphous state of the art at Warner Brothers. *Navy Blues*, starring Jack Oakie and Jack Haley, and *You're in the Army Now*, with Phil Silvers and Jimmy Durante, both attempted to capitalize on the new interest in war-theme films. They were actually the same musical, only the cut and color of the uniforms were different. Both concerned two hapless dupes drafted into the armed forces, and the troubles they caused their superior officers. Although ostensibly comic in form, each film displayed a few moments of serious intent. In *Navy Blues* Ann Sheridan explains to a naval gunner that it is unpatriotic for him to give up the navy in order to return to his farm in Iowa. *You're in the Army Now* also allows Durante and Silvers to explain the importance of the newly enacted selective service laws in song:

> The draft has begun
> I'm number two-eighty-one,
> I'm glad my number was called.
>
> Just like my dad
> When my dad was a lad,
> I'm glad my number was called.

These musicals seem a rather meretricious mistake, and despite the patriotic moments, they were the last films at Warners to make light of the armed forces. *Yankee Doodle Dandy* (1942), both for its popularity and excellence, confirmed Warners' commitment to musicals of patriotic thought and support for the war.

Film producers had sought the rights to Cohan's life since the beginning of the war. M-G-M at first seemed to have the inside track, as Cohan agreed to write the script and appear briefly in the film. The deal soured when Cohan insisted on final script approval. Shortly thereafter, William Cagney, James' brother, brought the idea to the attention of Jack Warner. The Cagneys had been seeking an ideal vehicle for James ever since Burton Fitts, a former Los Angeles District Attorney, had called the movie star a communist during his campaign for re-election. William Cagney told Jack Warner that "they should make a movie with Jim playing the damndest patriotic man in the whole world, George M. Cohan." The Cagneys hoped that this film would settle the question of James' patriotism once and for all. Cohan was paid $100,000 and given final script approval. The Cagneys and filmwriters Julius and Phillip Epstein ultimately ignored Cohan's desire to approve the script, and tinkered with it daily. Cohan became irate when he discovered what was happening, but William Cagney calmed him, urging him to wait and see the rough cut of the film. When Cohan came out of the projection room, he shook hands with Cagney and said, "You're all right!"[2]

Despite the particular motives for the production of the film, *Yankee Doodle Dandy* continued the strong support that the Warners' films had given to the current wartime situation. From the first moments of the film, as George M. Cohan visits Franklin Roosevelt to receive the Congressional Medal of Honor, a contemporary sense pervades a film that is essentially historical.

The film's major ballet, which is adapted from the Cohan stage musical *George Washington Jr.*, demonstrates this tension between present and past. The ballet presents a montage of images of America at war, which, according to Cagney's Cohan, shows that "the spirit of freedom is American." First the heroes of the American Revolution appear, marching with fife and drum in their fight for freedom. Next the Civil War is evoked, with slaves singing "Glory, Glory, Hallelujah," and Lincoln proclaiming that "government of the people, by the people, and for the people shall not perish from the earth." Images of the Spanish-American War and Teddy Roosevelt follow, and the music changes to "When Johnny Comes Marching Home Again." The scene then shifts to the "present," when Cohan explains that the common people must "stand united in peace and war" for "our country 'tis of thee." Father Cohan (Walter Huston) appears as Uncle Sam and mother (Rosemary De Camp) as the Statue of Liberty. The whole chorus carries flags, and a giant American flag is flashed on a scrim on the theater stage.

The music lends power to the strong patriotic fervor of the film. "You're a Grand Old Flag" and "Over There" allow Roosevelt to comment to Cohan that "your songs were weapons as strong as cannons and rifles in World War I." As George leaves the White House, soldiers going off to war sing "Over There." The time is the present, and all wars seem to blend and be dwarfed by the current conflict. The message is an urgent plea for a patriotism similar to that practiced by George M. Cohan.

Even the marketing of *Yankee Doodle Dandy* manifested the film's support for American wartime policy. The New York City premiere sponsored a war bond sales drive. Bonds were purchased in amounts from $25 to $25,000. Once the viewer purchased the bond, the tickets for *Yankee Doodle Dandy* would be free. Al Jolson bought the first $25,000 bond. The Hollywood premiere netted $5.8 million, enough to build three of the Liberty cargo vessels then under construction at California shipyards and begin a fourth ship. All donors found their names inscribed on scrolls placed in the captain's cabin on each of the three ships.[3]

This Is the Army (1943) continued the patriotic strains of *Yankee Doodle Dandy.* Only here Jack L. Warner went one step further. Not only would the film actively support American war policy on the screen, but also in the box office, as all profits would be donated to the Army Emergency Relief Fund. Warner estimated that the fund would receive between $5 million and $10 million dollars from the domestic distribution returns. Warner Brothers also contributed the services of Jack Warner (executive producer),

Hal Wallis (associate producer), and Michael Curtiz (director). In return the army supplied talented Hollywood actors enlisted in its ranks, such as Lieutenant Ronald Reagan and Private Joe Louis. Additionally, the army mounted an extensive advertising campaign:

> Whenever possible, military and civic patriotic ceremonies are being planned in connection with the premieres. Wednesday night in New York the Army staged a show of the men and equipment of modern war. About 400 men were in the colorful display, with anti-aircraft guns, a band, a camouflage unit, jeeps, and trucks. A detail of U.S. Army men, with two trucks, were assigned to distribute window display material on the picture to 8,000 stores in the five boroughs of New York.[4]

Variety also noted that "all railroads, buses, and subways in New York City" donated advertising space free of charge. Chase National Bank also provided "the Wrigley sign in the heart of Times Square."[5]

The film resurrected familiar themes which had proven successful in previous Warners' wartime efforts. Screenwriters Casey Robinson and Captain Claude Binyon adopted the use of the historical wartime metaphor. The first third of the film concerns the American entry into World War I. Terry Jones (George Murphy) and His All-Star Review are performing in vaudeville as the hoofer receives an ominous telegram while he is performing "Wait 'Til I'm Married to My Sweetie." Murphy is not alone in receiving a draft board summons. Maxie Twardofsky (George Tobias), a Jewish grocer, and Eddie Dibble (Charles Butterworth), a coronet player, are also drafted.

The army brass encourages Murphy to use his dancing talent and produce an army show *Yip Yip Yaphank*, which was actually written by Irving Berlin in 1917. Murphy demonstrates his sagacity as a producer by including such songs as "Beautiful Me, I'm on K.P." ("Against my wishes/I wash the dishes/To make this world safe for democracy."), but cutting "God Bless America" ("it's too slow"). This may seem a humorous decision, but Irving Berlin admitted to eliminating the song from the show and shelving it until 1938.

On opening night the stage troupe is summoned to Europe. Instead of performing the finale as planned, they march in formation from the theater as the audience cheers. ("It's real! They're going!") Murphy is injured in France and returns home before the Armistice. But the battle for freedom is not ended. The scene switches to a map of Czechoslovakia and Poland in flames. The bombing of Pearl Harbor is shown in vivid detail. As the oldsters from World War I listen to the news on the radio, their young sons decide to enlist.

When the youths, led by Ronald Reagan, report for duty, they too are urged to put on a show:

"A new war needs a new show."

"What will we call it?"

"Why not state the simple fact? *This Is the Army!*"

In this fashion Berlin's World War II army show is transferred to the screen. Interestingly, the creators of the film felt that they could not present the show itself. Rather, it is patterned after the Warner formulae developed after 1939. In addition to the use of historical metaphor, the screenplay introduces a variety of subplots designed to show how all resistance to the war effort is systematically eliminated. A mother who is embittered because of her son's early death realizes that everyone must support the war in order for the United States to win. Reagan is angered at first that he must stage a show while others are fighting in Europe. But, he, too, eventually realizes that everyone can contribute to the war effort in his own way.

Berlin's classic score furthers the patriotic intent by praising everyone involved with the war: "How About a Cheer for the Navy?", "American Eagles" (the Air Corps), "This Is the Army," and "What the Well-Dressed Man in Harlem Will Wear," a "tribute to the Negro soldier." For the show's finale, World War I and World War II are again dramatically linked as fathers and sons sing "This Time Is the Last Time," a rousing march which envisions a free world without the hardships of war.

David Butler's *Thank Your Lucky Stars* (1943) revealed how the consciousness of the war had altered the Warners' musical. Ostensibly, this star-studded revue seemed to have little or nothing to do with the contemporary situation. The slimmest of plots concerned Joan Leslie and Dennis Morgan, who try to audition for Eddie Cantor's benefit performance *The Cavalcade of Stars*, which featured all of Warner's top stars from Bette Davis to Errol Flynn.

While the plot remained an unintentional parody of the "backstage musicals" of the 1930s, the Arthur Schwartz and Frank Loesser songs seemed unable to escape the pervasive wartime psychology in their music. For example, Dinah Shore appears as a Southern belle during the Civil War. She sings goodbye to her lover, explaining that "it's a uniform first and love second" in "this mixed up world of 1861." She hopes that when he returns "we'll be living in a better world."

Errol Flynn follows with one of his few adventures in song, "That's What They Jolly Well Get," a melodic explanation of how he destroyed Nazi regiments and Japanese submarines. Bette Davis then contributes "They're Either Too Young or Too Old," a rhapsodic view of the home front. Since "there is no secret lover, the draft board didn't discover," Bette is forced to date prepubescent teens or doddering old men. She laments: "What's good is in the army, what's left cannot harm me." The prolific Eddie

Cantor appears in the finale singing "We're Staying Home, My Baby and Me, Doing the Patriotic Thing."

Hollywood Canteen (Delmar Davis, 1944) attempted to capitalize on the popular soldier canteens of the West and East coasts run by the stars of Hollywood and Broadway. *Hollywood Canteen* was really *Thank Your Lucky Stars* in khaki. Once again all of the stars in Warners' stable had been corralled into the film. As a result, the film canteen featured more celebrities than the real Hollywood Canteen ever could.

The melodies parallel those of *Thank Your Lucky Stars* but they have an added dimension. The concept of war in the previous film was generally abstract. Dinah Shore sang of the Civil War, Flynn was dressed as an English pirate, and Davis' song was a melodic form of lost love. In *Hollywood Canteen*, the songs assume an active and patriotic stance. Consider Dennis Morgan's "You Can Always Tell a Yank":

> You can always tell a Yank,
> By the way he drives a tank,
> To defend a thing called democracy,
> And save the world from tyranny.
> He's the kind of guy
> Wants a Yankee Doodle Deal
> Loves his apple pie and his Constitution.
> He's the kind of guy with a lot of sock appeal
> And he hates to heil or heel.*

While the participants in *Thank Your Lucky Stars* seemed concerned only with a successful charity show, the stars of *Hollywood Canteen* desire the end of the war. Everyone participates in this effort. On an individual level, the Andrews Sisters sing "I'm Getting Corns for My Country,"

---

*"You Can Always Tell a Yank" © 1944 Warner Bros. Inc. Copyright renewed. All rights reserved. Used by permission.

by doing a "patriotic jitterbug" for the soldiers. The Golden Gate Quartet explains in "The General Jumped at Dawn" that "all races and creeds, white men and black men" are "out to win the war" in an "all-American team effort."

Hollywood Canteen was one of the last Warners' musicals produced during the war. Busby Berkeley directed *Cinderella Jones* somewhat later, but its release was delayed until after the war. As a result almost all references to World War II were eliminated. A convoy of tanks appears in the last few seconds of the film in order to drive the young heiress (Joan Leslie) to the army chaplain so she may marry in time to receive a million dollar inheritance. Otherwise, what remains of the film is totally unrelated to the war.

Both *Rhapsody in Blue* and *Night and Day*, biographies of George Gershwin and Cole Porter, respectively, were conceived during the latter months of the war and heralded a new cycle of motion pictures concerning the lives of composers and lyricists. Yet, even *Night and Day* spends an inordinate amount of time in the French battlefield with Cole Porter during World War I, despite the fact that the film ostensibly has little to do with wartime themes.

The film claims that one of Porter's immortal song hits was inspired on a lonely French battlefield in 1915. While awaiting his orders, Cole overhears a black soldier humming and playing his bongo drums. This melody supposedly provided the genesis of Porter's classic "Begin the Beguine." Thus, the war apparently could have beneficial results for the young composer. This biographical license, however, was pure poppycock. Actually, the song first appeared in the Broadway musical *Jubilee* in 1935. Moss Hart recounts a slightly different version of the song's origin: "I suddenly recalled the time I had first heard it sung by Cole Porter himself, sitting at the upright piano in his cabin as the boat sailed towards the Fiji Islands."[6]

Despite the unusual liberties taken with these composer biographies, some facts remained intact. Both Porter and Gershwin met tragic fates. Porter's legs were crushed in a horse riding accident, and Gershwin's life ended at thirty-nine because of a brain tumor. These sour endings belie the notion that musical comedies are or should be "happy" in nature. Musical tragedy is a more fitting term for many of the musical films appearing during wartime. The Warners' productions were no exception.

A common theme unites the diverse musical productions presented by Warner Brothers during World War II. Each film stresses the importance of group unity. If this solidarity is ever broken, only disaster can occur. As a result, collective heroes and heroines dominate the films of this period. James Cagney is a member of the Four Cohans, Durante and Silvers are buddies in *You're in the Army Now,* and Haley and Oakie are partners in trouble in *Navy Blues.* Corporal Slim Green refuses to accept his weekend in a posh hotel in *Hollywood Canteen* unless his pal Sergeant Nolan (Dane Clark) can "bunk with him."

As long as the pals stick together, all remains rosy. However, if the unit is threatened by dissolution, disaster inevitably strikes. *Yankee Doodle Dandy* provides the best example. Once young George M. is successful on Broadway, he brings his family to New York to join his act. The Four Cohans of vaudeville days are resurrected and business booms. After years of success, George's parents decide to retire, and his sister resolves to marry. When George hears of his sister's plans, he notes: "The Four Cohans minus one Cohan equals nothing." These words are prophetic; George's world collapses as soon as the group splits up.

As a result, the tone of the film abruptly changes. Although a swift montage of marquee titles shows that Cohan produced and wrote his most successful plays between 1918 and 1928, scriptwriters Robert Buckner and Edmund Joseph ignore his triumphs. From the moment the Four Co-hans break up only the bitter aspects of George's life are shown on the screen. First George tries to answer critics who argue he can only write frothy musicals. He prepares *Popularity*, a drama, which is panned by the reviewers. Immediately thereafter George learns that the *Lusitania* is torpedoed. He tries to enlist, but he is too old. His sister dies, and in a lengthy episode, his father expires on screen. George severs relations with producer Sam Harris, who encouraged and aided George throughout his career. Cohan finally retires to a Connecticut farm. Near the end of the film a group of teens stop by to chat. They have never heard of Cohan or his famous songs. George does receive the Congressional Medal of Honor for his World War I songs, but this hasty happy ending hardly mollifies George's violation of the "unity principle." The implicit message of the film (but not necessarily of George's *real* life) is that the break-up of his family brought disaster into his life.

The two loners of the Warners' musicals receive the bitterest end. Both Porter and Gershwin ignore the importance of friendship and are continually berated for it. Joan Leslie refuses to marry Gershwin: "He has to go his way alone. He must be free." Alexis Smith also criticizes the composer of "Rhapsody In Blue": "You don't need anyone or anything." Alexis also portrays the wife of Cole Porter. Here, too, a normal marriage is impossible as Cole devotes too much time to his work and ignores his wife and her desire for a family. The loners are thus unlucky in friendship and love. This, in turn, dampens the usually gay musical comedy spirit and turns it strident.

Warners was not alone in this presentation of the importance of a collective hero who maintained unity and confraternity at all cost. The relatively frequent appearance of this theme would seem to dictate more than a mere imitation. The unavoidable conclusion remains that these films presented a message to America at war: "United We Stand, Divided We Fall."

In this fashion the musicals from the Warners' studio concentrated on a single theme from 1940 to 1945. Every musical comedy, whether operetta, all-star review, or stage adaptation, considered wartime themes. This mobilization in terms of content was followed by changes in style. The wartime musical was pared to the bone. The choreographic excess of Busby Berkeley and his imitators disappeared by 1940. No dancing pianos, no swimming pools, no swooping cameras, no dazzling chorines. Under the tutelage of LeRoy Prinz, dance director during this period, the Warners' musical could have been staged on the head of a pin.

Prinz's background for the task of dance director was unusual, to say the least. Although his grandfather had taught ballroom dancing and etiquette to the youth of St. Louis since 1887, young LeRoy had other goals in mind. At age sixteen he ran away from a Jesuit boarding school in Kansas City and hopped a train to New York. A young black, already on board the freight, stole LeRoy's fortune of twenty-five cents. As the long ride to the Big Apple continued, the two became unlikely friends and performed in the saloon circuit as "Prinz and Buck" in 1911.

Shortly thereafter, Prinz shipped off to France as a cabin boy. Once he arrived in France, he traded his knowledge of the American street steps in exchange for food and lodging. Later, he joined the French Foreign Legion as a bugler.

His expertise as a pilot was legendary. He survived fourteen crashes and carried a silver plate in his head to "commemorate" the last one. While convalescing, he organized shows for the troops. He later became an aviation instructor for the Mexican government and drifted to Nicaragua, where "he carried ammunition by plane and occasionally dropped some small bombs."

When the American Marines landed in Nicaragua, Prinz found it prudent to retreat to New York. He soon began staging ensemble numbers for such Broadway musicals as *Fioretta, My Marilyn,* and *Great Day.* Cecil B. DeMille summoned Prinz to Hollywood as a director in 1931 at $1,500 per month.[7]

Prinz's military background is comparable to that of Busby Berkeley, who also staged shows for American troops during World War I and later on Broadway. At this point, all resemblance ends. Prinz reversed every innovation that Berkeley had pioneered.

Berkeley's camera had broken the boundaries of the stage. Once the curtain rose on a Berkeley musical number, all consciousness of the stage disappeared. Prinz, however, resurrected these limits, and the audience is never allowed to forget it is watching a dance performed on a stage. Consider *Yankee Doodle Dandy.* When young Cohan first performs his hit song from *Little Johnny Jones,* the stage always intrudes. One shot features the orchestra pit, the next, the right wings, the boxes, the left wings, or the border of the curtain. Rarely does the camera forget its origins and participate in the dance numbers as Berkeley's once did. The camera is static. It behaves as a member of the audience, rather than as a member of the chorus.

Why blame Prinz? Others might criticize the director of the overall film, who might control such matters as camera placement. Prinz's problem stemmed from the fact that he was a dance director, not a choreographer. He utilized simple steps and dance routines. For that matter, so did Busby Berkeley. However, for Berkeley, the camera furthered the choreographic design. Once camera participation was lost, the pedestrian quality of Prinz's dance numbers is painfully revealed. No matter the picture, no matter the director, Prinz's dances are invariably the same, static and stagebound.

Dismissing Prinz as unimaginative would hardly be to the point. In general, de-emphasis on dance is a stark characteristic of the wartime musical. The hallmark of the Warners' musical of the forties is a return to reality. The thirties' musical had only flirted with the real world. Once the curtain lifted, fantasy could be given free reign. With the coming of war, the musical became limited in scope and insistent on reality.

For example, ask anyone what a film musical is. Invariably, the answer will detail a vision of people singing and dancing through the streets. (This is often used as an excuse by people who do not want to *see* a musical). This was untrue throughout World War II at Warner Brothers. Only once in six years does an unmotivated song occur, when Dennis Morgan and Joan Leslie sing in a cafeteria in *Thank Your Lucky Stars*. In every other instance the song is performed on a "stage"—whether in a nightclub, a theatre, or even a backyard.

The same realistic bent which dominated the themes of the Warners' wartime musicals also determined the form. Songs were limited to their most rational status, performed only on a stage in front of an audience. As a result, the Warners' films remain the sparsest of the age. Yet, at the same time, they became the most reflective of the current trend in the Hollywood musical which looked away from fantasy to a world of reality—a world at war.

PART THREE

THE MUSIC

5

From "Blues in the Night" to "Ac-cen-tchu-ate the Positive": Film Music Goes to War

While the producers, directors, stars, and screenwriters committed themselves to the winning of the war, the composers and lyricists of the Hollywood musical appeared somewhat bewildered by the swiftly changing events on the international scene. How could their music help the war effort? President Roosevelt had given music a lofty position in the mobilization for war, claiming that it "could help to inspire a fervor for the spiritual values of our way of life, and thus strengthen democracy against those forces which would subjugate and enthrall mankind."[1] Yet, despite the president's enthusiasm, songwriters remained at a loss as government agencies harshly criticized their initial efforts at wartime music.

Lyman Bryson, head of the Music Committee of the Office of War Information, complained constantly about the latest popular tunes. He found contemporary ballads too saccharine, noting that current war songs "were just love songs with a once-over-lightly war background." Lyricists merely slipped a soldier into their songs, but as Bryson explained, "it was still boy-meets-girl stuff."[2] Bryson also resisted the unbridled optimism of the first rash of war songs. With such ditties as "We'll Meet Again," "The White Cliffs of Dover," and "Blue Skies Are Just Around the Corner," he feared that the listening audience would be lulled into a sense of security.[3]

Another OWI spokesman explained that the best war song thus far had been "Der Führer's Face," which gave Hitler a resounding Bronx cheer in a Donald Duck short. He explained: "Maybe this new ditty isn't exactly the suavest thing, but it's certainly right down to the ground. We want to give Hitler a more audible razzing than we've been doing. We've concentrated too much on hating the Japs when our number one menace is still Schickelgruber, the [Charlie] Chaplin of Berlin."[4]

The ultimate goal became the manufacture of "freedom songs." After an analysis of Goebbel's use of music for propaganda purposes, the OWI urged songwriters to "wave the flag and shout Hallelujah for all conquered and oppressed peoples."

If the goals of war music were so clearly marked, why the confusion and why the difficulty? Why were there not more songs of a martial nature during the first years of the war? The OWI again supplied the rationale: "The one-step and two-step of 1917 made possible a host of spirited martial songs such as 'Over There,' 'K-K-K-Katy,' 'Hinky Dinky Parlez-Vous,' 'How You Gonna Keep 'Em Down on the Farm?' and others. The major problem was that the 1940 audience preferred the fox-trot or swing." Furthermore, the OWI argued, the active public of World War I had turned passive, since the radio partially supplanted the need to attend dances in order to hear the latest music.

The OWI seemed pressed for a solution to this dilemma. There was talk of asking "Fred Astaire or Arthur Murray to invent a fashionable new rip-snorting patriotic style of stepping that would span the bridge from 1918 to 1942" so the United States would "become more oompah and militaristic."[5] The discussions with these dancing greats never came to fruition, but the conversations of the OWI and memories of the glorious music of the past war seemed to prod songwriters into action.

In the first years of the war, movie musicals continually looked back to the successful manner in which earlier songwriters had tackled the mobilization of society in time of war. A cursory glance at the musical films of the period might lead one to assume that George M. Cohan was the most prolific film composer during World War II, instead of Harold Arlen or Irving Berlin. *Yankee Doodle Dandy* was the most prominent example. M-G-M bought the Cohan play *Little Nellie Kelly* and refurbished it into a Judy Garland musical. Judy and Mickey Rooney portrayed Faye Templeton and George M. Cohan in *Babes on Broadway* (1941), singing such Cohan hits as "Yankee Doodle Dandy" and "Over There." "Over There" also graced *Four Jills and a Jeep* (1944), and "Give My Regards to Broadway" appeared in the *Great American Broadcast* (1941). Actually, Cohan, who had just emerged from retirement to appear in Rodgers and Hart's Broadway musical *I'd Rather Be Right*, had little to do with the revival of his songs. His musical numbers fulfilled two important functions. First of all, they supplied the patriotic war songs that Washington claimed were of the utmost necessity. Secondly, the use of old songs took the pressure off Hollywood studios to develop a stable of composers and lyricists comparable to that of the 1930s within a short period of time. Indeed, by 1939, when the musical reached its nadir, Hollywood dismissed the popular songwriters of the 1930s and was unable to fill the gap at such short notice. Not until 1942 was a new generation of Hollywood composers operating at full capacity.

Cohan was not alone in Hollywood's search for the music of bygone days. Among the songs admired by the OWI, "K-K-K-Katy" reappeared in *Tin Pan Alley* (1940), and *For Me and My Gal* revived "How You Gonna Keep 'Em Down on the Farm?," as well as "What Are You Going to Do to Help the Boys?" for the trio of Judy Garland, George Murphy, and Gene Kelly.

Perhaps Irving Berlin made the most fortunate rediscovery. He recalled his experience in the camp show *Yip Yip Yaphank* in 1917, and remembered that he had written a patriotic finale for the show. The song was so patriotic that Berlin felt that it might be a trifle excessive for the all-soldier show. The song remained unpublished until 1938. In that year Berlin returned from London after the Munich Pact and felt compelled to write a patriotic song, but he composed nothing that satisfied him. He remembered the old song that he had written and revised it slightly, giving it to Kate Smith to sing. "God Bless America" became one of the most successful songs of modern popular music. Berlin established a trust fund for the Boy Scouts and the Girl Scouts of America from the royalties. Within one year the scouts received over $50,000. The scouts were chosen as recipients because, as Herbert Bayard Swope explained, "their completely nonsectarian work was calculated to best promote unity in mind and patriotism, two sentiments that are inherent in the song itself." Even the Democrats and the Republicans wanted to use the song for their convention theme in 1940.[6]

Other Irving Berlin World War I hits were also revived. He performed "Oh How I Hate to Get Up in the Morning" in both the stage and film versions of *This Is the Army*, the World War II successor to *Yip Yip Yaphank*.[7] Rumor has it that an electrician overheard Berlin's rendition of the song and commented to a friend: "If the guy who wrote this song could hear the way this guy is singing it, he'd roll over in his grave." "Mandy," written in 1917, also found its way into the film version of *This Is the Army,* as did the classic "God Bless America."[8]

In this revival of past songs much of the original meaning was lost as lyrics had to be updated for present-day audiences. Perhaps the most humorous incident concerned the patriotic sounding Gershwin tune "Strike Up the Band." Despite the seemingly contemporary flavor of the song, it actually came from a 1927 musical of the same name which closed out of town. Morrie Ryskind softened the original George S. Kaufman libretto which was a vicious satire on international politics, the League of Nations, and war itself. This less acerbic version of *Strike Up the Band* reopened on Broadway in 1930. At this time "Strike Up the Band" was an antimilitary march:

> We fought in nineteen-seventeen,
> Rum-ta-ta tum-tum-tum!
> And drove the tyrant from the scene,
> Rum-ta-ta tum-tum-tum.
>
> We're in a bigger better war
> For your patriotic past-time.
> We don't know what we're fighting for—
> But we didn't know the last time!

By 1940, this viewpoint seemed highly impolitic for the film version. Ira Gershwin revised the lyric for this pre-Pearl Harbor musical to read:

> We hope there'll be no other war,
> But if we're forced into one—
> The flag that we'll be fighting for
> Is the Red and White and Blue one!

The finale of the 1940 film version of *Strike Up the Band* ends with Mickey Rooney and Judy Garland superimposed against the flag for which they would gladly fight.

The song underwent further revisions as the war progressed. A 1942 version assumed a more vehement tone:

> Again the Hun is at the gate
> For his customary past-time,
> Again he sings his Hymn of Hate—
> But we'll make this time the last time.*

Recently Ira Gershwin voiced the hope that this later edi-
tion had gone out of print.[9]

Despite a general acceptance of the World War I approach to patriotic music in the first years of the war, this
procedure eventually became self-defeating. After all, composers' trunks have a bottom. The *New York Times* began
to criticize the "Proustian spirit that has been brooding
over the creative acres of Hollywood."[10] The Music War
Committee (MWC), an independent group of Broadway,
Hollywood, and popular-song composers and lyricists
reached similar conclusions. The executive committee of
the MWC argued: "Forget about 6/8 tempos and World
War I. Today's songwriters should stop writing for the
1917 war. They should adapt their patriotic and military
ideas to the 1943 pattern of show business and showman-
ship."

The MWC's instructions to songwriters amounted to a
complete reversal of the OWI approach to wartime melodies, which seemed opportune at a time when the OWI
had been deprived of all domestic operations by the U.S.
Congress. First of all, the MWC urged its members to assume a positive approach in their writing. "Forget the
frustration of the 'Maybe I will lose my girl' or 'Is my girl
back home two-timing me?' songs," it argued. Similarly,
the MWC suggested that the songwriters not fret about

---

*"Strike Up the Band," by Ira Gershwin and George Gershwin. © 1927 New World Music
Corporation. Copyright renewed. All rights reserved. Used by permission of Warner Bros.
Music.

the "lights going out all over Europe, but sing of the victory to come." Oscar Hammerstein II earned harsh criticism on this point. The MWC believed that he should not have written "The Last Time I Saw Paris," the Academy Award winner from *Lady Be Good* in 1941. A more optimistic outlook would have led to "The Next Time I See Paris."[11]

It was hoped that this new approach to songwriting would produce successful World War II songs, instead of mere reprises of World War I ditties. Irving Berlin commented that the "Over There" of World War II had yet to be written: "It will be written and when it comes you will know it. Maybe orchestra leaders don't like to play war tunes, but they'll play the big hit when they get it."[12]

In general, songwriters did not resist the attempt to use their music and lyrics in support of the war effort. E.Y. Harburg and Ira Gershwin explained this philosophy in a Harold Arlen song "If That's Propaganda (Make the Most of It)":

The whole wide world is in danger
As the Axis hacks away.
There's a mad dog in the manger
And he must be brought to bay.

Shall we who still know freedom
Just stand by and be dumb?
Or shall we help to save the world
From those who would enslave the world?

Let's get out of the woods.
Let's deliver the goods.

Rush the rations to Russia!
Put the pressure on Prussia!
If that's propaganda,
Make the most of it!

Propaganda, yes!
But for a world we used to know.*

In many respects, Irving Berlin was the leader in the search for relevant and contemporary songs. Although he revived his World War I song hits on many occasions, he also possessed a keen sensitivity to current wartime events. Although there are no classics of a "God Bless America" caliber here, Berlin's songs for the American government revealed that music might play an important role in the war effort.

Secretary of the Treasury Morgenthau asked Berlin to write a song which would encourage the sale of war bonds. The resultant tune, "Any Bonds Today," was freed from all copyright or royalty restrictions so that the "song may be used by anyone at anytime and place" and thus increase bond sales.[13] Even the Australian government adopted the song for use in their war austerity loan campaign. Berlin followed soon after with "Angels of Mercy," the official Red Cross song.[14] Again at Morgenthau's request Berlin wrote "I Paid My Income Tax Today," which explained to American citizens the importance of their tax dollars to the war effort.[15]

Berlin's first attempt to integrate a patriotic song in a film musical came with *Holiday Inn* (1942) directed by Mark Sandrich. Bing Crosby's cozy little inn opened only on national holidays, and July Fourth provided an appropriate time for a song celebrating American virtues. The "Freedom Song" was dedicated to "all people who strive to be free" and the song provided a musical listing of all the freedoms proclaimed in the Bill of Rights. Although the lyrics made no direct reference to the current war effort, the accompanying visual montage supplied the necessary link. A backdrop behind Bing displayed the Statue of Liberty, planes and battleships, General MacArthur, and FDR. The final image is that of the American flag. A star-spangled curtain is lowered, and the song is ended.[16]

While the "Freedom Song" from *Holiday Inn* directly considers the war issue, "White Christmas" is mentioned more often as the ideal wartime song. One critic noted: "It was indeed a song in the wartime mood, a bit sad and yearning—an emotion with which both homesick soldiers and civilians could identify."[17] Ironically, Berlin never intended the song to have such a meaning: "It came out at a time when we were at war and it became a peace song in wartime, nothing I ever intended."[18]

While Berlin might compose a song as current as the daily newspaper, composers and lyricists of film musicals faced a certain difficulty. Songs composed for films might not reach a viewing audience for months, and, as a result, the topicality strived for in Berlin's government songs was usually impossible. Berlin himself hated this lag between composition and audience approval, and, for this reason, claimed that he preferred Broadway to Hollywood musicals. Despite this lack of immediacy, film musicals attempted to turn their attention from World War I to World War II, and, by 1943, to explain the contemporary world situation to American film audiences.

While the Music War Committee urged its members to take an optimistic stance, events from Europe buoyed the spirits of composers and lyricists. By the end of 1943 Mussolini had fallen, Allied troops were on the attack in Europe, and the war in North Africa seemed over. At last there seemed to be a basis for hope. The songs of this latter period of the war reveal dreams of a brighter day to come in the Hollywood musical. Harold Arlen converted from "Blues in the Night" to the perky "Ac-cent-tchu-ate the Positive" for *Here Come the Waves*. Ira Gershwin and E.Y. Harburg combined their lyrical talents to urge the world to "Make Way for Tomorrow" in *Cover Girl*. Ethel Merman raised her ample voice in *Stage Door Canteen* (1943) to sing a prophetic "Marching Through Berlin," as though the war had already been won:

> We'll be singing Hallelujah
> Marching through Berlin
> The devil put on a different face
> Came to plague the human race
> We'll put that old devil back in his place
> Sing Hallelujah!

Although the war had brought long separations and had disrupted the romances of countless young men and women, even the tone of the romantic ballads seemed to soften. In the early days of the war, these songs expressed anxiety and concern, as soldiers worried whether their women would wait for them, and the women worried about their men returning alive. "Don't Sit Under the Apple Tree with Anyone Else But Me" was appropriately one of the most popular songs of 1942. A year later mooning hymns to a distant love seemed to be taken less seriously. Perhaps the best example of this trend was Ray Bolger's rendition of "The Girl I Long to Leave Behind" in *Stage Door Canteen*. The Lorenz Hart lyric describes a young woman who is "less refined than Lou Costello":

> She has hair she wears like Veronica Lake
> So that fifty per cent of her is blind.
> She is known to her daddy as "mother's mistake,"
> She's the girl I long to leave behind.

In keeping with this optimistic trend the armed forces experienced a glorification which has never been equalled. Virtually every branch of the fighting forces received a song from noted songwriters which extolled their virtues. Berlin praised the men on the ground and the men in the air ("American Eagles") in *This Is the Army,* but then he self-consciously added "How about a Cheer for the Navy?" as though he realized that he had forgotten something of great importance. Cole Porter also contributed "Glide, Glider, Glide" as well as "Sailors of the Sky." Musicals of the period even claimed that "It's a Swelluva Helluva Life in the Army" *(Hey, Rookie).*

Interestingly, the aura of hope pervaded those songs which concerned events occurring away from the home front. However, as the songs approached subject matter closer to home, the optimism seemed to fade as if the daily sacrifices that each citizen made for the war effort seemed to stand in the way of the romantic ideals of the songwriters. Somehow "Co-operate with Your Air Raid Warden" *(Priorities on Parade)* or "He Loved Me Till the All-Clear Came" *(Star Spangled Rhythm)* lacked the glamor of the songs which preached optimism in the course of war. Love no longer seemed as cheerful in the minds of lyricists as rationing, government bureaucratic hassles, shortages, and the black market pervaded the world of musical comedy films dealing with domestic life. Phil Silvers, as the master of ceremonies in Danny McGuire's Brooklyn Night Club, explained the situation in *Cover Girl:*

> But—no complaining
> Through the campaigning;
> Don't ask what's in the ragout.
> All rationed by the OPA
> Is heaven and U-toe-pee-a—
> So long as they don't ration
> My passion
> For you.*

---

*"Who's Complaining" by Jerome Kern & Ira Gershwin. Copyright © 1943 T. B. Harms Company. Copyright renewed. c/o The Welk Music Group, Santa Monica, Calif. 90401. International copyright secured. All rights reserved. Used by permission.

Bette Davis explained the difficulties of yet another curious shortage in *Thank Your Lucky Stars*. She wanders lonely through the streets of a small town, and stares wistfully at a huge Victory poster with pictures of virile representatives of the army, navy, and marines. She is alone now, because "there is no secret lover, the draft board didn't discover." Now all the men "are either too young or too old." The Arthur Schwartz-Frank Loesser song presents Bette with a strange alternative; she must date men below the age of puberty or men so old that she must carry them around the dance floor.

Thus the songs of the wartime period provide a vivid tableau of life on the home front. While songs of "escape" may have characterized the first years of the war, musical comedy composers eventually turned their attention to the events at hand, and expressed the contemporary situation in song by displaying a definite commitment to the wartime effort. As a result, the so-called "escapist" musical of the early 1940s actually reflected changing wartime society and encouraged patriotic support of the American soldier. Therefore, in form and in theme, the musical escaped its frivolous image in a time of national emergency.

6

"The Joint Is Really Jumpin' Down at Carnegie Hall": Operetta at War

Operetta and musical comedy coexisted peacefully during the first decade of the musical film. Each genre developed its own talent and style. While Hollywood producers looked to Broadway for musical comedy talent, the creators of the operetta sought singing talent at the Metropolitan Opera. Lawrence Tibbett, Grace Moore, Dennis King, and John McCormack dominated these early efforts, while Jeanette MacDonald and Nelson Eddy remain the best remembered by modern audiences. After their successful *Naughty Marietta* (1935), this renowned team appeared in a successful series of classic operettas: *Rose Marie* (1936), *Maytime* (1937), *The Girl of the Golden West* (1938), *Sweethearts* (1938), *New Moon* (1940), and *Bitter Sweet* (1940).

The coming of World War II to America brought an end to the MacDonald and Eddy partnership and a marked decline in the popularity of the operetta. This illustrious team appeared together on the screen only once more, in 1942, in Rodgers and Hart's *I Married an Angel*, a film version of

71

the recent Broadway hit. Audiences abandoned the operetta with a surprising swiftness, thus ending a thirteen year
film cycle.

Unlike the film musical, the operetta remained resistant
to change. Based on turn-of-the-century models, the film
operetta became a stubborn anachronism as the film musical converted to a wartime mentality. While musicals considered the plight of the soldier, the operetta remained
mired in mythical plots of medieval Ruritania or the distant Canadian Rockies. *Broadway Serenade*, produced by
MGM in 1939, encapsulated the plight of the operetta in
a period of change.

As Nelson Eddy went his own way in *Let Freedom Ring*,
Jeanette MacDonald appeared solo after a lengthy series of
operetta hits. *Broadway Serenade*, as the title indicated, was
not a standard operetta, but a musical comedy. Ostensibly,
Jeanette appeared in this new film to bridge the widening
gap between musical comedy and operetta, a formidable
task. Unfortunately, from the first moments of the film, the
operatic aspects were overshadowed by standard musical
comedy fare.

Timmy Allen (Lew Ayres), a frustrated classical pianist,
needs a thousand dollars so he and his wife Mary (Jeanette
MacDonald) can study music in Italy for a year. He resolves to prostitute his talent and hack out a popular song
which he believes will make money. He revamps a Tchaikovsky melody (Nur Wer die Sehnsucht Kennt, Opus 6,
No. 6) into "For Ev'ry Lonely Heart." Timmy and Mary
call Mr. Collier (Frank Morgan), a prosperous Broadway
producer, and request an audition. He is too busy, but the
show's chief angel Larry Bryant (Ian Hunter) spots the
beautiful Mary and insists that Collier let them perform.

The audition becomes a shambles, as Mary's song is continually interrupted by Mr. Collier. "For Ev'ry Lonely
Heart" bores Collier. Finally, he askes Mary to "swing

it." She is annoyed by the request, but Timmy urges her to do it for the money. This attempt is also interrupted as the peripatetic choreographer, Gene (Franklin Pangborn), threatens to strangle the current star of *Collier's Revue of 1939* because she sings "Flying High" straight, instead of swinging it. Seeing her chance, Mary swings "Flying High" for the group, and Collier hires her on the spot.

Mary's rendition of "Flying High" makes her the toast of Broadway, but her true vocation wanes. In the realm of the stage musical, opera or operetta seemingly have no place. As a result it becomes more and more difficult to integrate the operatic arias for which Jeanette MacDonald is so well known. Gene, the choreographer, at last discovers a solution to this problem:

GENE: Mary, Mary! I've got it! I've got it! I've got it!

MARY: Good. Now if you take it somewhere else, we'll all be happy.

GENE: No levity now—I've got to work out this idea right away. Where's the piano?

MARY: Would you mind telling me what this is all about?

GENE: Why, your Madame Butterfly number. Mr. Collier wants an alibi for grand opera in a revue. So, with my new lyrics I'll tell them that the world is shifting, restless, ever changing, and then—boom—we'll sock 'em in the puss with Butterfly. Now for the lead up:

Time is a magic thief,
Changes joy to grief,
Makes you laugh and weep . . .

Has Jeanette MacDonald ever needed such complicated logic just to sing "Un Bel Di"? After the boys sing "Time Changes Everything," Mary is at last alone on the stage and able to sing an aria from start to finish without interruption. This is no mean feat as the finale to *Broadway Serenade* clearly demonstrates.

Mary has still not been able to complete "For Ev'ry Lonely Heart." The song was ripped to shreds in the audition. Perhaps it can be presented without problems in the finale. Unfortunately, Mary will not be struggling with the song alone in the finale of *Broadway Serenade,* but also with the creative excess of Busby Berkeley, recently plucked from the Warners' studios. Berkeley reinterprets the song to the extent that Mary is never able to finish it. The words "lonely heart" stick in her mind, as she repeats them over and over while faced with the barrage of the Berkeley ballet corps.

At first, "For Ev'ry Lonely Heart" is a simple peasant's melody. A herdsman plays the tune for his flock of sheep. A composer, obviously Tchaikovsky, overhears the melody and arranges it into "For Ev'ry Lonely Heart." Mary begins to sing the song, but she is unable to get beyond the words "lonely heart." She sings from a lofty pedestal and looks down at masked dancers. These grotesque masks bear faces with exaggerated smiles. The dancers swing "Lonely Heart" without a care in the world. Only Mary remains without a smile.

Suddenly, the pedestal disappears and Mary remains alone, dressed in white, against a dark backdrop. Black jitterbugs arrive and try to force Mary to join their modern dance. She resists and tries to sing "For Ev'ry Lonely Heart" in a purely classical style. Once again, she can only repeat the words "lonely heart."

A dancer with a white mask arrives. He too forces Mary to join his dance. Mary again resists, but the bopster is too smart for her. He grabs a smiling caricature mask of Jeanette MacDonald and forces it on Mary's face. She thus appears to enjoy the modern music and she begins to jitterbug. But this is a clever ruse, for she seizes the first chance to escape.

Mary is at last alone. She stands on a new pedestal miles above the other dancers. Below, the band plays a 1939 version of "For Ev'ry Lonely Heart," but Mary is at last free from the bane of this popular swing music. "The End" flashes on the screen.

Berkeley's finale has been criticized as excessive, but it is certainly symbolic of the tensions between the operetta and the musical comedy in the war years. Jeanette, alone on her pedestal, refuses to follow the trends of modern music. As a result, she falls from the mainstream of popularity by insisting on her old-fashioned ways. Berkeley sees this isolation as self-destructive. The ideal is to change with the times. There is nothing inherently wrong with swinging Tchaikovsky.

Berkeley and the writers of *Broadway Serenade* are not the only ones to criticize the growing isolation of the operetta from the rapidly changing world. All classical music comes under suspicion as Nancy Walker and June Allyson proclaim the "Three B's" as outmoded. They prefer "boogie-woogie, barrelhouse, and the blues" in *Best Foot Forward* (1941). Eleanor Powell's three B's become "ballet, buck and boogie-woogie" in *Thousands Cheer* (1943). Bach, Beethoven, and Brahms are passé as Judy Garland explains in "The Joint Is Really Jumpin' Down at Carnegie Hall" in the same film. Poor José Iturbi is unable to finish a chord without Judy interrupting with a boogie-woogie beat:

Millions have heard you play Chopin.
The critics applaud and approve.
But millions more would simply adore
To hear you get in the groove.

Judy explains to José that times have changed:

Instead of Strauss, they play Irving Berlin
Instead of Brahms, it's "Begin the Beguine",

Those classic "yackies" are due for a fall,
The joint is really jumpin' down at Carnegie Hall.*

As classical music takes a back seat to pop, swing, jazz, and boogie-woogie, the film operetta is faced with an impossible dilemma: change or die. But what can be changed? Swing the music and the operetta disappears. The music cannot be tampered with. The only solution becomes to modernize the libretto. Hopefully, by stop-gap means the operetta might survive on film. Thus, like the Hollywood musical, the operetta also turned to the problems of America at war.

The wartime operetta abandoned the mythical kingdoms of the past and considered topics of current importance. *Rio Rita* (1942) became an Abbott and Costello vehicle which concerned the attempt of Nazi spies to smuggle bombs into the United States from a Mexican border hotel. All that remained of the original score were a few songs for Kathyrn Grayson.

Desert Song (Warner Brothers, 1943) revamped the original operetta in a singularly clever fashion. The new version opens in Geneva in 1939 where "a few men of good will held back the straining dogs of war while others under an innocent guise were still trading with the enemy." "The North African Trading Company," a French concern, is sending arms shipments to North Africa. The weapons find their way into German hands and they are used against the Riffs, a group of desert bandits, who are hindering the progress of a trans-African railroad under German control. The Germans wish to use the Riffs as cheap labor, while the Riffs desire to remain free. As the bandit leader El-Kabar explains, "The Riffs are savages, but they are savages about their freedom."

---

*"The Joint Is Really Jumpin' in Carnegie Hall" by Ralph Blane, Roger Edens, and Hugh Martin. Copyright © 1943, renewed 1971, Metro-Goldwyn-Mayer Inc. All rights administered by Leo Feist, Inc. All rights reserved. Used by permission.

El-Kabar is none other than Dennis Morgan, an American bandleader. When summoned on dangerous missions, he dons a cape and becomes the mysterious El-Kabar. At first it seems odd that a bandleader would be chosen as the leader of a group of desert tribesmen. Yet, *Desert Song* demonstrates that Morgan has several useful skills. As a musician, Morgan knows countless numbers of songs. Each song has a ritual meaning to the Riffs, and, in turn, they dictate a prearranged course of action. This system of song-codes is quite necessary as the Riffs are continually followed by French and German spies.

One evening Morgan is entertaining the Riffs in his nightclub. He learns from informers that there will be a raid on the club that evening. He conveys this information to the Riffs by singing the classic Sigmund Romberg ballad, "One Alone." The Riffs pretend to hate the song, and one-by-one, they leave the nightclub. Morgan is truly "One Alone" by the time he finishes the song. Since the Riffs escape, the raid is a failure.

In this fashion, many of the songs from the original operetta are retained in the film version of *Desert Song*. The Romberg melodies become coded forms of communication in this new libretto. Thanks to this oblique rationale, the songs remain.

The finale of *Desert Song* parallels *Casablanca*. The French General cooperates with El-Kabar, who has discovered documents which link Nazi money to the trans-African railway. El-Kabar trusts him because "France is a democracy." The scheme is revealed, and the Riffs retain their freedom.

The Nazis are apparently everywhere in 1942 and 1943. Even Jeanette MacDonald attempts to thwart their plans in *Cairo* (M-G-M, 1942). German agents, led by Lionel Atwill, Mona Barrie, and Edward Ciannelli, have discovered a new robot plane which can be sent on bombing missions anywhere in the world. From deep inside an Egyptian tomb the Nazis plan their first attack—a U.S. naval transport. If that mission proves a success, then the Suez Canal is next, and ultimately the Allied powers themselves. At first, the Nazis manage to remain well hidden in tombs or behind walls. The doors to their secret hiding places can only be opened by a special tuning fork which hits a high C note when it is struck. This clever gimmick proves to be the Nazis' undoing.

Homer Smith (Robert Young), a war correspondent for the *Cavity Rock* (California) *Times-Leader*, accidentally draws Marcia Warren (Jeanette MacDonald) into this web of intrigue. For a variety of reasons, the gullible Homer suspects that Marcia is a Nazi agent. One day she walks into a jewelry shop. While examining the merchandise, Marcia sees a small white mouse run across the room. Marcia screams and unbeknownst to her, a sliding panel opens in the back of the store. Homer sees what occurs, and concludes that Marcia is definitely a Nazi spy. The shopkeeper comments in shocked amazement, "Are you in the habit of screaming a perfect high-C?" Marcia replies that she never screams flat, and she leaves the store.

Homer eventually falls in love with Marcia, and, despite the evidence, he decides that she cannot be a spy. He then follows the Germans to the pyramids by riding on the back bumper of their car. The spies spot Homer in the rear view mirror and plan a swift demise for the American bumbler. Homer overhears the German's comment that the American is too stupid to try to escape in the waiting airplane. Homer jumps at the chance to escape and hides in the plane. Unfortunately, he does not realize that this is the robot airplane which will soon be sent on a suicide mission.

Marcia finds a note from Homer and summons British Intelligence to her aid. They arrive at the tomb and find no clues of the Nazis' whereabouts. Marcia discovers a few hundred dollar bills scattered at the entrance to the tomb. What are hundred dollar bills but "C notes"? Marcia recognizes the clever message and sings a high-C. Nothing happens. She admits that she may have been a trifle flat. She tries again and the door to the tomb opens, revealing the German spies. As the agents seize the spies, Homer at last understands what has happened to him. He uses his necktie as a fuse, explodes the bombs in mid-air, and parachutes from the plane. The Nazi plot is foiled. Homer wins a movie contract and marries his beloved Marcia.

As Dennis Morgan's "One Alone" performed a function in *Desert Song,* Jeanette MacDonald's high-C also saves the day in *Cairo.* Yet, these attempts to modernize the operetta were too little and too late. The convoluted plots constrained the performers as no operetta had ever done before. The music lost its place of prime importance, and the operetta became doomed. *Cairo* was one of Jeanette MacDonald's least popular pictures. Perhaps the title preordained its failure. The film was released after the Cairo conference with Roosevelt, Churchill, and Chinese and Turkish leaders. A musical version of a wartime conference certainly seemed an improbable affair. Yet, these attempts at defensive modernization could not save the operetta. It fizzled to a halt after 1943, and Jeanette MacDonald and Nelson Eddy appeared in grade-B films for the rest of the decade. They, too, were the victims of the popular wartime musical comedies.

PART FOUR

MEN AND WOMEN

7

The Soldier
as a Song and Dance Man

As the war continued, the uninvolved civilian disappeared from Hollywood, both on screen and in real life. The draft and voluntary enlistments devastated the movie kingdom's supply of leading men, as James Stewart, Robert Montgomery, and Douglas Fairbanks, Jr., reported for duty. Directorial ranks diminished as the Signal Corps paged Frank Capra, William Wyler, and John Huston. Hollywood briefly faced a manpower crisis and scraped the bottom of the barrel for substitute actors, especially those with a 4-F rating.

The civilian actor also vanished in musical films of the wartime era. Gone was the plethora of actors, dancers, singers, composers, lyricists, and choreographers who had populated the backstage musicals of the previous decade. Conscription reached the imaginary world of the film and replaced the uncommitted civilian with the singing and dancing soldier. Had the majority of these musicals been shot in color, the dominant motif would have been khaki and olive green, as the enlisted man became the new hero of the wartime musical.

This trend was not only true of musical comedies. Early in 1940, *Variety* noted the flux of films concerning wartime: "Springing to the bugle call of the United States War and Navy Departments for aid in enlisting public opinion on the side of conscription and national defense, Hollywood's film studios are making wide revisions in already announced 1940–1941 features to include a flock of films to whip up enthusiasm for preparedness and the draft. Work on them is being rushed whenever possible."[1]

Variety also congratulated Warner Brothers for leading the "patriotism list" with five features. This trend demonstrated that Hollywood had openly proclaimed its support for the war effort. There remained no attempt to hide its intentions as had occurred during the Senate investigation of 1939: "A few weeks ago studios were loath to admit that anything they were turning out could possibly be classed as propaganda. Now, with reps of the government on the coast in confabs with producers, there's no longer any hiding of the purpose of certain films, which is evident from a title like 20th's *Yankee Doodle Goes to Plattsburg*. All of these pictures, however, will naturally have a generous coating of "escapist" story to preserve their palatability."[2]

Hollywood's turn to wartime themes has generally been recognized in both its dramas and comedies. But the musical comedy also contributed to the war effort by the depiction of the honest and committed soldier eager to fight and die for his country. Unlike the majority of wartime films, the soldier of the musical comedy was rarely seen overseas in a combat role. There were no instances of privates dancing over foxholes and singing the praises of the submachine gun. With the exception of a fleeting glimpse of soldiers in the South Pacific in *Hollywood Canteen* and *Up in Arms* (1944), the soldier of musical comedy fame remained on the home front. Three themes dominated these films: (1) the process of conscription; (2) the one, two, or three day pass; and (3) the camp show. Each plot provided an ample variety of songs and dances which invariably portrayed the same message: the civilian must be willing to fight for his country.

This homily was conveyed to musical comedy audiences by the presentation of three standard varieties of soldier: (1) the reluctant soldier, who is originally embittered about being drafted, but eventually sees the light; (2) the timid soldier, who although shy and awkward, is able to save the day for the American forces; and (3) the committed soldier who understands his country's values and is willing to fight for them. Each breed of soldier seemed to appeal to members of the film audience who faced the war with a sense of ambivalence. "Should I enlist?" asked the viewer. "Yes!" answered the musical comedy.

The wartime career of Gene Kelly best demonstrates the role of the reluctant soldier who is eventually convinced of the righteousness of his country's position. Interestingly, Gene Kelly's conversion is not completed within a single film. His musical comedies reveal a gradual progression. In 1942 and 1943 Gene betrays bitterness and ambivalence towards a war that is interrupting his career and private life. Only by 1945, ironically the last year of the war, does Kelly display an active support of the war effort from the beginning of a film to the end.

Gene Kelly began his singing and dancing career on Broadway. As a member of a six man chorus, he supported Mary Martin in her show-stopper, "My Heart Belongs to Daddy" in *Leave It to Me* (1938). Shortly thereafter he was chosen to portray Broadway's most famous heel in Rodgers and Hart's *Pal Joey* (1940). Within a year the young hoofer was brought to Hollywood and catapulted to stardom in *For Me and My Gal* (1942). His partner was the now adult Judy Garland, who had graduated from the Mickey

Rooney films to portray a vaudeville performer during
World War I.

For Me and My Gal was easily the most depressing musical Hollywood had yet produced. Gene Kelly won the du-
bious distinction of portraying the first musical draft
dodger. Kelly meets Judy Garland in a small midwestern
town. He plays his new song for her ("For Me and My
Gal"), and they immediately become partners. Kelly is
haunted by the all-absorbing goal of playing the Palace.
Years later, as Gene finally receives his long awaited chance
to hit the big time, World War I intrudes and he is called
to enlist. Since he is a dancer, Kelly decides to mangle his
hand in a trunk, so he will be declared ineligible. Judy Garland discovers his actions and leaves him. With the act dissolved and a withered hand, Gene's chances of playing the
Palace fade.

Apparently, preview audiences found the plot depressing and distasteful, as 85 percent believed that George Murphy, the vaudevillian who enlisted, should have married
Judy. Twenty-one days of retakes attempted to make Gene
Kelly a hero.[3] In the final version of the film, Kelly moves
to France to entertain the troops in a USO show. One night
he singlehandedly leads a convoy of American ambulances
through German-occupied territory. He realizes the error
of his ways, becomes a hero, and wins Judy's respect and
love.[4]

Yet, Kelly does not learn his lesson for his next film,
Thousands Cheer (1943), which once again presents him as
the reluctant soldier. Gene, a lowly draftee, is embittered
because the army has interrupted his career as "Eddie
Marsh and the Flying Corbinos," his family's circus aerialist act. Worse yet, the army has taken a man who loves the
air and has placed him in the infantry. Kelly is also annoyed by the rigid hierarchy of the wartime army: "Privates don't mix with officers or their families because we're

not good enough." Kelly attempts to transfer to the air corps, but his request is denied by the colonel because he has no sense of "discipline or morale."

Gene Kelly accidently meets Kathryn Grayson at the local train station and falls in love with her. Unfortunately, she is the colonel's daughter and is not permitted to fraternize with privates, and especially Kelly. However, the father softens and explains that he might reconsider if Kelly "learns discipline."

Kelly tries to obey the army's rules since he loves Grayson, but he cannot wait. He attempts to elope, but is thwarted by zealous military police. He is summarily tossed into the guardhouse while shouting: "Tell 'em what happens when a soldier falls in love with brass!"

Kelly is released from jail for the camp show, since he promised that he would appear with "The Flying Corbinos." As the aerialists rehearse for the big show, Gene discovers that his timing is slightly off. His sister almost falls to the net below. She criticizes him, "You haven't been good lately. Where is your teamwork?" His father also responds, "It's a long drop from here—it's a good thing I'm at my post." At this moment Gene realizes the importance of teamwork and discipline. Being an aerialist is like being in the army. If everyone does not work together, the results can be disastrous, even deadly. In order to emphasize the importance of "teamwork," he decides to perform without a net. If he does not think of others, he will certainly fall to his death.

Kelly has learned his lesson. He survives and faces a court martial. He explains that he wants "to be the most important man in the world—a private in the U.S. Army." He tears up his transfer papers and is shipped out with his regiment. The colonel finally sees Kelly's worth and allows his daughter to become engaged before the troops leave. Thus, in *Thousands Cheer*, Kelly learns the importance of discipline in the wartime army, as he is converted from a reluctant to a committed soldier.

Cover Girl (1944) reveals a new Gene Kelly. He is still embittered, but this time it is because he cannot fight overseas. After six months in Libya, Kelly was "shot up" and sent home to recuperate. He wants to participate, but now he is physically unable. As a substitute, he teams with Phil Silvers and entertains in local USO shows.

Only by 1945 does Kelly appear as actively committed to the war effort in *Anchors Aweigh*. This is somewhat ironic since Kelly was called by his draft board during the production of this film. He claimed that he was "ready to go," but he stalled in order to complete the Jule Styne-Sammy Cahn musical. Kelly worked "night and day" to finish the film before he had to report, and the most troublesome sequence concerned a combination live action and cartoon dance with Jerry the Mouse, of Tom and Jerry fame. Gene filmed his dance steps first, and then Hanna and Barbera supplied more than ten thousand pictures of the mouse in action. The sequence was completed faster than expected, and Kelly reported for duty before the film was released.[5]

In *Anchors Aweigh* Kelly is a hero from the moment the film begins. José Iturbi conducts the navy band as the troops march in formation. A general turns to Iturbi after the performance and thanks him for his performance. Iturbi responds, "But it is I as an American citizen who should thank you!" One of the people the general praises is Gene Kelly, to whom he gives a Silver Star and a four-day pass for bravery in the Pacific fighting. Thus, by 1945, Kelly has learned that there is no place in the army for a reluctant or embittered soldier. In order for the American way to prevail, everyone must do his part for the war effort.

The second major type of soldier in wartime musicals was the timid soldier, the Casper Milquetoast, who believed that he could never participate in the manly activities of the U.S. Army. He was shy, he was weak, and he was often 4-F.

Many musical comedy heroes of this ilk were often so physically and mentally unsound that they would not be accepted in the army. Abbott and Costello in *Rio Rita* and Red Skelton in *I Dood It* (1943) portray civilians, but manage to thwart Nazi spy rings in their own confusing manner. They may not be army material, but they still manage to display their heroism on the homefront.

Other 4-F's desire to enlist, but the army will not accept them. Fred MacMurray goes to extraordinary lengths in *Where Do We Go from Here?* (1945) to join the marines. He enlists the aid of a bumbling magician to help him achieve his goal: "The magician misses by a few hundred years and gets him first into Washington's Revolutionary Army, aboard Columbus' ship, and then in Dutch New Amsterdam, before landing him in the Marines."[6] Despite all this effort, the war was practically over by the time this film was released.

Danny Kaye best represents the timid soldier, shy, confused, and 4-F, in *Up in Arms*. He portrays Danny Weems, war hero, who has recently captured "twenty Japs" as the film begins. "But," as the narrator explains, "he wasn't always this fearless." The scene changes to a Staten Island draft board where Danny's file is being examined. He is an acknowledged physical wreck. He has "flat feet and raised arches" and "nervous digestion and nervous indigestion." Danny is also deathly afraid of germs, and leaves public places for fear of contagion. The draft board decides that he is a hypochondriac, and it changes his status to 1-A. Danny receives his draft notice and begins to cry.

He and his best friend Dana Andrews are sent overseas. Danny blunders continually and spends most of the journey in the brig. Even after the ship docks in the Pacific, Danny remains incarcerated. He is unexpectedly "saved" by a platoon of Japanese soldiers who raid the guardhouse. They wish to know the number of Allied forces, ships, and planes in the area. Danny accidentally overpowers the Japanese commander and dons his uniform. He slants his eyes and shouts nonsense phrases in pseudo-Japanese. Danny unintentionally shouts "Follow me" in Japanese, and the troops line up to follow their leader. Danny leads the troops into an ambush and captures the whole platoon singlehandedly. As a result of his "brave" efforts, Danny becomes a war hero.

In this fashion the timid soldier demonstrated to the audience that anyone can become a hero, no matter how meek or physically uncoordinated. After all, if Abbott and Costello or the hypochondriac Danny Kaye can become a successful soldier, then anyone can. There is, therefore, no need for any civilian to be frightened about entering the armed forces.

The majority of the soldier-entertainers were committed military men with a pride in their uniform and a sense of mission. They had no doubts about their role in the armed forces of World War II, as this song from *Hey Rookie!* (1944) demonstrates:

> It's great to be in uniform
> In khaki, blue, or gray I look grand.
> It's great to be in uniform
> The best dressed man in the land,
> (Made by your Uncle Sam).

Who represents the committed soldier? It is hard to imagine someone manly enough to fill the bill. Some might suggest Dennis Morgan, who sings "You Can Always Tell a Yank" in *Hollywood Canteen*. Actually, the most consistently heroic is none other than Fred Astaire. At first, this may seem paradoxical. Although an excellent singer and dancer, Astaire seems ill fitted for the role of committed soldier. He is somewhat short, slim, and frankly too aristocratic. The top hat and tails would seem out of place in the trenches. Yet, despite these drawbacks, the nimble Fred Astaire is attributed some of the most glorious and heroic exploits performed by musical military men in the wartime films.

Fred had a brief experience in the armed forces as a sailor in *Follow the Fleet* (1936). He abandoned his tuxedo for most of the film, except for the nightclub number "Let's Face the Music and Dance." But this was a peacetime performance, and Fred returned to his standard attire in *Swing Time,* also released in 1936. Yet, with the coming of the war in Europe, Astaire is one of the first to surrender his dancing shoes. The joyful dancing of Fred Astaire and Ginger Rogers is starkly interrupted by the coming of war in *The Story of Vernon and Irene Castle* (1939). This is the last Astaire and Rogers film for RKO, and the ending is indeed prophetic. Astaire is the first star killed in action in a musical film.

The first two-thirds of the film is in the light-hearted style characteristic of the RKO musicals. After a chance meeting at Coney Island in 1911, Vernon (Fred) marries Irene (Ginger), a young dancer. The new team travels to Paris and develops the Castle Walk, which soon becomes America's hottest dance craze. Although the Castles are at the peak of their success, Vernon, an English citizen, joins the Royal Flying Corps after the outbreak of World War I. Vernon escapes unscathed from battles in France, but he is killed in a training flight accident after his return to the United States. The film ends with a "Phantom Dance," as Irene waltzes with the ghost of her late husband.

Astaire then enters the army in his next film *You'll Never Get Rich* (1941). Here his motives are slightly less exalted than in 1939. Fred is about to be shot by Rita Hayworth's brother as the draft notice arrives. "The army is the solution to all my problems," claims Fred as he adroitly weasles out of a breach of promise suit. Fred is so intent on entering the army as a means of avoiding a domestic squabble that he places a five pound sinker under his hat so he will not be found underweight. Fred's behavior in the army differs little from his life as a civilian. As a matter of fact, he spends most of the film in the guardhouse.

This capricious behavior disappears by 1943 as Fred becomes a war hero in *The Sky's the Limit*. As fighting ace Fred Atwell, he is given a ticker tape parade when he returns to the United States. He is a pilot of such great renown that he is sent on a series of personal appearance tours from coast to coast. During this period he meets the young Joan Manion (Joan Leslie). Fred wants Joan to love him on his own merits, not because he is a war hero. As a result, he masquerades as a jobless and cynical aristocrat. Joan refuses to give him the time of day since she believes it is more important to entertain the boys who are actually fighting the war. Nevertheless, her disdain eventually turns to love. Only then does Fred reveal his identity, just moments before he is to embark on a new mission. He kisses Joan, and his squadron flies off. Joan can now be proud of the man she loves.

The military musicals of this period thus portray a standard message. No matter who you are, Kelly, Kaye, or Astaire, the musical comedy experience will convert you into the soldier par excellence. Bitterness fades and shyness disappears once the citizen enters the army. The film musical of the 1940s, with the soldier as the central figure, became a giant enlistment poster, encouraging American citizens to either enlist or accept the draft without resentment or fear. The prototypes of Kelly, Kaye, and Astaire were not the he-men glorified in such films as *Action in the North Atlantic* (1943), but common men lending their services to the American war effort. This fact encouraged au-

This Is the Army finale. (Museum of Modern Art/Film Stills Archive). *See p. 49.*

Walter Huston as Father Cohan in *Yankee Doodle Dandy*. (Wisconsin Center for Film and Theater Research). *See pp. 44–46.*

Cohan's chorus girls in *Yankee Doodle Dandy*. (Wisconsin Center for Film and Theater Research). *See pp. 44–46.*

Images of war in "George Washington Jr. Ballet" in *Yankee Doodle Dandy*. (Wisconsin Center for Film and Theater Research). *See pp. 44–46.*

"I've worked the land and it's mine," explains Lionel Barrymore to Edward Arnold in *Let Freedom Ring*. (Museum of Modern Art/Film Stills Archive). *See pp. 34–35.*

Images of war in "George Washington Jr. Ballet" in *Yankee Doodle Dandy*. (Wisconsin Center for Film and Theater Research). *See pp. 44–46.*

"How About a Cheer for the Navy?" from *This Is the Army*. (Museum of Modern Art/Film Stills Archive). *See p. 69.*

Irving Berlin sings "Oh, How I Hate to Get Up in the Morning" in *This Is the Army*. (Museum of Modern Art/Film Stills Archive). *See p. 62.*

An intimate party on the Cole Porter estate in *Night and Day*. (Wisconsin Center for Film and Theater Research). *See p. 51.*

Max (Reginald Owen) introduces Ann Sothern and Robert Young's "tender and affectionate salute to a lost city," "The Last Time I Saw Paris" in *Lady Be Good*. (Museum of Modern Art/Film Stills Archive). *See pp. 36–39.*

Ann Sothern sings "The Last Time I Saw Paris" in *Lady Be Good*. Robert Young is the accompanist. (Museum of Modern Art/Film Stills Archive). *See pp. 36–39.*

Joe E. Brown and Dennis Morgan sing "You Can Always Tell a Yank" in *Hollywood Canteen*. (Museum of Modern Art/Film Stills Archive). *See pp. 50–51.*

Fred MacMurray is declared 4-F in *Where Do We Go from Here?* (Museum of Modern Art/Film Stills Archive). *See p. 89.*

George Murphy trains the World War I troops in *This Is the Army*. (Museum of Modern Art/Film Stills Archive). *See pp. 46–49, 62, 69.*

Fred Astaire and the Delta River Boys in *You'll Never Get Rich*. (Museum of Modern Art/Film Stills Archive). *See p. 124.*

Fred Astaire in *The Sky's the Limit.* (Museum of Modern Art/Film Stills Archive)

Fred Astaire in *The Sky's the Limit*. (Wisconsin Center for Film and Theater Research). *See p. 92.*

Bing Crosby sings "Old Glory" in *Star Spangled Rhythm*. (Museum of Modern Art/Film Stills Archive). *See pp. 100–101.*

Gene Kelly, Phil Silvers, and Rita Hayworth sing "Make Way for Tomorrow" in *Cover Girl*. (Museum of Modern Art/Film Stills Archive). *See pp. 67–69.*

Virginia Wilson, Phil Silvers, and Rita Hayworth sing "Who's Complaining" in *Cover Girl*. (Museum of Modern Art/Film Stills Archive). *See pp. 67–69.*

Jeanette MacDonald sings "For Every Lonely Heart" in *Broadway Serenade*. (Museum of Modern Art/Film Stills Archive). *See pp. 71–75.*

Fred Astaire and Ginger Rogers in the "Phantom Dance" in *The Story of Vernon and Irene Castle*. (Museum of Modern Art/Film Stills Archive). *See pp. 146–47.*

Kathryn Grayson and Gene Kelly in *Anchors Aweigh*. (Museum of Modern Art/Film Stills Archive). *See p. 88.*

Jerry the Mouse and Gene Kelly in *Anchors Aweigh*. (Museum of Modern Art/Film Stills Archive). *See p. 88.*

Red Skelton in *Bathing Beauty*. (Museum of Modern Art/Film Stills Archive). *See p. 101.*

Nancy Walker on the swing shift with Ben Blue in *Broadway Rhythm*. (Museum of Modern Art/Film Stills Archive). *See p. 94.*

n the Swing Shift" with the cast of *Star Spangled Rhythm*. (Museum of Modern Art/Film Stills chive). *See pp. 100–101.*

Betty Hutton in *Here Come the Waves*. (Museum of Modern Art/Film Stills Archive). *See p. 67.*

Kay Francis, Martha Raye, Carole Landis, and Mitzi Mayfair entertain the troops in *Four Jills in a Jeep*. (Museum of Modern Art/Film Stills Archive). *See pp. 140–41.*

Above and below. Gene Kelly and Kathryn Grayson in *Thousands Cheer.* (Museum of Modern Art/Film Stills Archive). *See pp. 86–88.*

Mary Martin sings "My Heart Belongs to Daddy" in *Night and Day*. (Wisconsin Center for Film and Theater Research). *See p. 51.*

Lena Horne and Eddie "Rochester" Anderson in *Cabin in the Sky*. (Museum of Modern A Film Stills Archive). *See pp. 124–127.*

Ethel Waters and Eddie "Rochester" Anderson in *Cabin in the Sky*. (Museum of Modern Art/Film Stills Archive). *See pp. 124–127.*

Busby Berkeley's "The Lady in the Tutti-Frutti Hat" in *The Gang's All Here*.
(Museum of Modern Art/Film Stills Archive). *See pp. 116–17.*

Carmen Miranda in *Springtime in the Rockies*. (Museum of Modern Art/Film Stills Archive).
See p. 112.

Carmen Miranda romances Cesar Romero in *Weekend in Havana.*
(Museum of Modern Art/Film Stills Archive). *See p. 115.*

Jeanette MacDonald (hiding in rear) discovers Nazi agents in *Cairo*. (Museum of Modern Art/Film Stills Archive). *See pp. 77–79.*

Dennis Morgan and Bruce Cabot search for spies in *The Desert Song*. (Museum of Modern Art/Film Stills Archive). *See pp. 76–77.*

Danny Kaye in *Up in Arms*. (Museum of Modern Art/Film Stills Archive). *See pp. 89–90.*

Margaret O'Brien (with long nose) in the Halloween sequence in *Meet Me in St. Louis.* (Museum of Modern Art/Film Stills Archive). *See pp. 150–52.*

Judy Garland comforts Margaret O'Brien in *Meet Me in St. Louis.* (Museum of Modern Art/Film Stills Archive). *See pp. 150–52.*

June Haver and Betty Grable as *The Dolly Sisters*. Sig Ruman and John Payne are their escorts. (Museum of Modern Art/Film Stills Archive). *See pp. 147–48.*

Gene Kelly and Judy Garland in *For Me and My Gal*. (Museum of Modern Art/Film Stills Archive). *See pp. 149–50.*

Dinah Shore entertains wounded servicemen in *Follow the Boys*. (Museum of Modern Art/Film Stills Archive)

dience identification with these musical stars, since they demonstrated the same emotions that preoccupied members of the film audience. The Hollywood musical explained and rationalized these fears, assuring the American citizen that serving the armed forces was both a necessary and useful experience.

8

"The Woman Behind the Man Behind the Gun"

As the diminutive Nancy Walker begins her solo number in *Broadway Rhythm* (1944), she pauses momentarily and asks herself, "What am I doing here? I could be earning money as a welder on the swing shift." She shrugs her shoulders, dismisses the thought, and begins to sing. This brief aside reveals a new insight into the wartime musicals. Previously, the giggling chorine thought of only two things, appearing in a successful show and snagging her man. Usually, by the film's finale, the heroine had achieved both of her goals. However, as Nancy Walker's comment reveals, these were no longer the only goals to which a woman might aspire. A more important issue was at stake by 1941—winning the war. In order to achieve victory, the musical comedy girl became a woman who outgrew adolescent fancies and faced the world in a time of harsh reality.

The new woman of the wartime musicals was stronger and more self-assured than ever before. She, too, could participate in the war effort as an equal with men. This was a realization that society at large had already faced. As men left for service abroad, women assumed their roles with consummate ease. They became welders, cab drivers, government workers, and tackled jobs that had formerly been presumed to be "men's work." Admittedly, they were not always paid the same as their male counterparts, but the wartime era marked an important step in eroding the rigid sex barriers which prevailed in many occupations.

The movie musical faithfully echoed society in this respect, as the dancing showgirls of the 1930s faded before welders and riveters on the American screen:

> Once they had so many dates life became a bore,
> Now they're in defense work making bombers by
> the score.
> They gave up their fancy clothes and are happy
> in navy blue,
> They are wearing cotton hose and are happy in
> khaki, too.

This song from *Melody Parade* (1943) reveals that women are no longer concerned with the frivolous things in life as they willingly undertake defense work. This message is repeated in film after film. *Star Spangled Rhythm* (1944) presents Betty Hutton proclaiming "I'm Doing It for Defense" and Marjorie Reynolds, Betty Rhodes, and Donna Drake singing of life "On the Swing Shift."

Rosie the Riveter (1944) further idealized the female defense worker. Rosalind "Rosie" Warren (Jane Frazee) delays her marriage so she can work in the aircraft industry. When her friend Vera asks when she will wed, Rosie replies, "I don't know—winning the war is more important." At first the male workers are reluctant to accept the women, but as Rosie and Vera learn their tasks they are greeted as equals. Only a tell-tale sign reminds the men of their new co-workers: "If your sweater is too long, look out for machines. If your sweater is too small, look out for the men."

The aircraft plant is honored for its contribution to the

war effort. Senator Johnson presents Rosie with an E
award (for excellence), and explains that she "typifies the
Miss America of today." As Rosie accepts the honor, her
boyfriend Charlie arrives in uniform. He asks Rosie to wait
for the duration and she willingly agrees.

As Rosie and Charlie embrace, the film presents the ultimate tribute to the new American woman. A soldier sings:

> While other girls attend their cocktail bars
> Sipping dry martinis and caviars
> There are other girls putting them to shame
> Rosie is her name.
>
> All the day long—whether rain or shine,
> She's a part of the assembly line.
> She's making history working for victory,
> Rosie the Riveter.
>
> She keeps a sharp lookout for sabotage,
> Sitting out there on the fusilage.
> That little frail can do more than a male
> can do,
> Rosie the Riveter.

The song continues as a female chorus enters carrying
model airplanes on sticks. The message implies that without these women the planes would not fly:

> When they give her a production E,
> She's as proud as a girl can be.
> There's something true about, red, white,
> and blue about
> Rosie the Riveter.*

This transformation of the status of the American
woman is not primarily a question of economics. Women

---

*"Rosie the Riveter" written by Redd Evans and John Jacob Loeb. Copyright © 1942 by
Paramount Music Corporation. Copyright © renewed 1969 and assigned to Paramount
Music Corporation.

lend their talents to the war effort in whatever way they can. Some join the armed forces as WAVES and WACS; others work for the Red Cross or the USO. Although the women are not fighting in the trenches, they are coming closer to the men in action than ever before:

> I'm going to be a commando
> And blitzkreig the land we call love
> I'm going to be a bombardier
> I'm going to drop kisses from above.
> I'll change the flashing eagle into a turtle dove
> We'll be Mr. and Mrs. Commando
> Who invaded the land of love.

The Hollywood musical celebrated the woman of the armed forces in such films as *Here Comes the Waves* (1944) and *Up In Arms* (1944). The latter film, a Danny Kaye vehicle, provides an interesting reversal. Here the women are superior to men. Dinah Shore portrays a WAC lieutenant to Danny Kaye's unfortunate private. Love vanishes in the modern army in the face of superior rank, as Danny is unable to kiss or even talk to Dinah since she outranks him. It is both a humiliating and frustrating experience for the private.

The new women are so committed to winning the war that romance becomes secondary. Judy Garland provides the best example in *For Me and My Gal*, discussed in detail in chapter 12. She is madly in love with Gene Kelly, but when she discovers that he has crippled his hand in order to avoid the draft, she refuses to see him. Gene must endure a lengthy penance, touring in USO shows in France. Only when he is awarded a medal for bravery in the line of fire does Judy consent to resume their relationship.

Joan Leslie faces the reverse problem in *This Is the Army*. She wants to marry Ronald Reagan, her long time beau, but he refuses. He does not want to go to war and leave her a widow. Reagan explains that his friend "Blake was killed at Pearl Harbor" and left his family alone and without support. Leslie at first agrees to his logic and decides to join the WACS for the duration. At this time she realizes the fallacy in Reagan's argument:

JOAN: You don't know what this war is about. We're
           a free people fighting to be free. Free to
           marry. Free to raise a family.
RONALD: I know that.
JOAN: Then why do you act as if we lost the war.
           Open your heart. We're all in this fight to-
           gether. Women as well as men sharing our re-
           sponsibilities. I want to be part of you—the
           part that goes with you on the battlefield.
           This is a free United States. If we want to get
           married—let's get married.

Joan tells Ronald they are getting married, and he accepts. Joan's female proposal certainly symbolizes a sharp reversal in traditional male and female roles.

This ambiguity in sex roles can be seen even in musical films which avoid all mention of war. The issue is exploited cleverly in *Sun Valley Serenade* (1941), which features Sonja Henie. Although the film features the Glenn Miller Orchestra and the song hit "Chattanooga Choo-Choo," Miss Henie does not belong to the musical in the traditional sense. Although neither a singer or a dancer, her choreographed figure skating enchanted audiences in several Twentieth Century-Fox films.

From the first moment of the film, confusion reigns. Ted Scott (John Payne), a piano player, discovers that his agent has arranged for the Immigration Department to send his client a war orphan. Begrudgingly, Ted agrees to this publicity stunt, only to discover that his Norwegian orphan is not a child, but a beautiful young woman, Karen Benson

(Henie). She is eternally grateful to Ted: "I am so happy to be here. Words cannot express your kind and noble action." Ted, however, is irate, since he knows his fiancee Vivian (Lynn Bari) will never understand the presence of this woman in his home.

The energetic sportswoman is an immediate enigma to Ted ("Didn't you ever think about pounding a typewriter or working in a beauty salon?"). He prefers Vivian, a wealthy, self-indulgent singer. She hates the band's latest booking in Sun Valley, since she despises cold weather, so she resolves to spend most of the time lounging in her room or in the heated swimming pool. The Sun Valley atmosphere, however, gives Karen a chance to show her talents to Ted Scott.

Although Ted loves to ski, he is somewhat repelled by Karen's skill on the slopes. She taunts him as he boards the ski lift: "Only a softy takes a lift when he can ski. Norwegians only take the ski lift when they are on a stretcher." She then proceeds to ski rings around the humiliated Mr. Scott.

Yet, as much as Ted is confused by this energetic young woman, he is also attracted to her. The pampered Vivian begins to lose esteem in his eyes. Eventually he realizes that he loves Karen, and they decide to marry. The film ends with a choreographed ice display with Sonja and hundreds of soldiers dressed in black who appear from nowhere in a token reference to the war effort.

Ted's ambiguous feelings toward Karen are partly based on the fact that she, the female, is the pursuer in this film. He feels trapped as a strong, talented, and energetic woman is able to beat him at sports and win him in marriage.

Ted Scott is not alone in this sexual confusion as traditional sex roles lose their meaning in this time of war. One of the prime characteristics of wartime musicals is the strong presence of transvestite comedy, as though males are seeking revenge for female attempts to invade their sexual domain. This is not a friendly transvestism, for it is pervaded by a sense of bitterness and mockery. This scene from *Star Spangled Rhythm* is revealing in this respect:

BOB HOPE: In these war times women are taking the place of men in almost every occupation. Well for instance, last night I had a lot of trouble with a woman taxi driver—she wanted me to sit in the back seat. However in this next scene we are going to show you how men are replacing women in this next sketch entitled, "If Men Played Cards As Women Do." We have four of our manliest men to give you a rough idea.

Bob Hope chooses to emphasize "manliest" to describe the men who perform in this skit. They mimic women who gossip, compare clothing and hair styles, and wear girdles to look thin. But, worst of all, they play cards as women do:

RAY MILLAND: Are the red chips worth more than the blue chips?

LYNNE OVERMAN: I don't know. Let's make 'em all worth the same thing.

RAY: Alright! A quarter of a cent apiece!

FRANCHOT TONE: But let's just pretend they're dollars.

LYNNE: That makes it more exciting.

RAY: A pinochle deck. Can you play poker with it?

FRANCHOT: Of course! We always use pinochle cards. We get better hands that way.

RAY: Oh. How many cards do I deal?

FRANCHOT: Five, I think.

LYNNE: Well, sometimes seven

FRANCHOT: Well, there's a nine card game, too.

FRED MACMURRAY: Yeah, but they call that baseball, don't they?

RAY: I think we can start out with five, huh?

LYNNE: Sure, we can play baseball later.

This one skit is not enough for *Star Spangled Rhythm*. It is preceded by Walter Catlett, Arthur Treacher, and Sterling Holloway doing parodies of Paulette Goddard, Dorothy Lamour, and Veronica Lake. Each skit betrays a bitterness at its base, as though the men are "getting even" for the female actions which threaten their identity.

Star Spangled Rhythm is not an isolated case. Whenever sexual frustrations occur the male star is apt to dress in drag for revenge. Danny Kaye, unable to kiss his WAC lieutenant girlfriend, borrows a woman's uniform in *Up In Arms*. Red Skelton in *Bathing Beauty* (1944) follows a similar tactic. When his beloved Esther Williams jilts him at the altar, Red follows her to a posh eastern girls' college. He discovers that the college bylaws do not prohibit male students, so he applies for admittance to the school. He is accepted, and then must attend all the courses required for women. Naturally, for ballet class he must dress in women's dancing clothes. Red eventually wins back his beloved, but not before he has assumed a traditional woman's role and blurred the traditional division between the sexes. Once again, a sense of revenge blunts the humor of the transvestite comedy for modern audiences.

Only one female missed the venom of these transvestite musical numbers. Carmen Miranda became the most easily imitated musical star by men and women alike. In such films as *Down Argentine Way* (Betty Grable), *Babes on Broadway* (Mickey Rooney), and *Winged Victory* (an air force sergeant), both males and females attempted Miranda impressions. The Brazilian's outlandish garb made her an easy mark for her followers.

Thus the wartime musicals tended to blur sex roles rather than reinforce them. As women assumed more prominent film roles, partly as a result of the absence of male stars who had enlisted or were drafted, their portrayals broke many of the sexual boundaries established during the 1930s. The men in the musicals did not react by attempting to reinforce their traditional roles. Rather, they became confused and disoriented in several of the movie musicals, often turning to transvestite humor as a form of revenge.

In some ways their attitudes parallel those of soldiers returning home after World War II or even after the Vietnam War. When these men arrived they expected their traditional prewar family life to be restored. However, they were unaware that many women had shed their domestic roles. They had had jobs and in many cases had run their families perfectly well during the husband's absence. Like the musical comedy men, the returning soldiers were also disoriented by this abrupt change in sexual roles and were often unable to accept it. This is not to suggest that real soldiers followed their musical comedy counterparts on the path to transvestism. Rather, both the real world and the musical world faced similar problems as the war undermined traditional assumptions about sexual roles and the family.

PART FIVE

VIEWS OF SOCIETY

9

Hollywood's
Good Neighbor Policy:
The Latin American Musical

Walter Lippmann once said that Americans would do anything for Latin America except read about it. This relative indifference becomes apparent in the analysis of stereotypes in American films before World War II. Despite the enormous cultural diversity within Central and South America, Latin American behavior was depicted as predictably uniform. The "greaser," or Mexican (the terms were synonymous), was a rapacious bandit bent on murder and destruction. Although clever in his evil ways, the Latin invariably failed to outwit the North American cowboy or seduce his woman.[1]

Official complaints from the Mexican government in the 1920s did little to prevent Hollywood from portraying the Latin in an unfavorable light. An embargo of companies that continued to perpetuate the "greaser" image proved considerably more successful, forcing studios to eliminate this unflattering image by the end of the decade. Hollywood, however, chose to ignore the Latin during the 1930s rather than compensate for the wrongs of the earlier era. Of all the major studios, only RKO, controlled by the Rockefeller family which also had considerable investments in Venezuela, attempted to portray a Latin society accurately.[2] *Flying Down to Rio* (1933) used native Latins in prominent roles while other studios still presented their contract artists as Latins by using brown-face make-up. Paul Muni thus became Warner Brothers' resident "Mexican" in both *Bordertown* (1935) and *Juarez* (1939).

The situation changed abruptly in 1939, and, all of a sudden, films utilizing Latin stars, historical heroes, and locales flooded American screens. Such eminent leaders as Benito Juarez and Simón Bolívar were immortalized on film. Talent scouts brought planeloads of Latin American talent to Hollywood, as viewers discovered and delighted in Carmen Miranda, Desi Arnaz, and Cesar Romero. Films also began to differentiate between varying South American locales, allowing viewers to spend a *Weekend in Havana* (1941) or travel *Down Argentine Way* (1940).

The reason for this deluge of films with Latin American themes might be partially attributed to deliberate government policy. With the growing threat of war with Germany, the United States appeared eager to ease any remaining tensions with South American governments in order to maintain hemispheric unity as a bulwark against foreign invasion. Roosevelt thus attempted to resurrect the "Good Neighbor Policy" which had been ignored in the 1930s in the face of the Mexican government's expropriation of American oil companies and American intervention in Nicaragua and Cuba. Anxious to smooth these differences, Roosevelt explained the basis for his vigorous reassertion of the Good Neighbor Policy:

I began to visualize a wholly new attitude toward other American Republics based on an honest and sincere desire, first, to remove from their minds all fear of American aggression—territorial or financial—and, second, to take them into a kind of hemispheric partnership in which no Republic would take undue advantage.[3]

While all government agencies were expected to support the official policy of inter-American unity, a major effort was expected from the Office of the Coordinator of Inter-American Affairs and its director, Nelson Rockefeller.[4] Rockefeller appointed a former associate and current vice-president of the Museum of Modern Art to head the motion picture section of this division. John Hay ("Jock") Whitney seemed an appropriate candidate for the position since he claimed to recognize the unique role of film in the promotion of inter-American understanding. He explained:

The Office of the Coordinator of Inter-American Affairs has a share in the task of imparting the full force of the meaning of freedom and sovereignty to a quarter of a billion people in the Americas. The menace of Nazism and its allied doctrines, its techniques and tactics must be understood from Hudson Bay to Punta Arenas. Wherever the motion picture can do a basic job of spreading the gospel of the Americas' common stake in this struggle, there that job must and shall be done.[5]

Similarly, the Hays Office, the MPPDA self-regulatory agency, also appointed an expert in Latin American affairs in order to avoid blatant errors which might offend the "neighbors to the South." Will Hays declared that the appointment of Addison Durland to this post would "be another step in the motion picture industry's cooperation in current events to promote hemispheric solidarity."[6] This was not mere hyperbole, since Durland, director of NBC's Spanish division, spoke the language fluently and held a degree from the Universidad Nacional de Cuba.

Although the activities of the motion picture section

were primarily regulatory, the office also participated in the production of several newsreels and short subjects.[7] Rockefeller and Whitney were instrumental in the hiring of Walt Disney "as the first Hollywood producer of motion pictures specifically intended to carry a message of democracy and friendship below the Rio Grande." Whitney claimed that Disney would show "the truth about the American way," and another executive proclaimed him "the greatest goodwill ambassador of all time." He added that "people all over the world know Disney and love his characters." Therefore, "they would believe Disney's message of Americanism."[8] Whitney also urged the Disney animators to create a new character, a Miss Pan-Americana, symbol of inter-American unity, but instead they provided Jose Carioca, the pugnacious Brazilian parrot who appeared in *Saludos Amigos* and *The Three Caballeros.*[9]

The Rockefeller office also sponsored the showings of Hollywood films with vigorous statements of the democratic way of life "in American embassies and ministries throughout South America." Thus, the Latin American "diplomatic circuit" saw such films as *Confessions of a Nazi Spy, Young Mr. Lincoln, Abe Lincoln in Illinois, Man Hunt,* and *Sergeant York.* It was estimated that more than 13,000 viewed the first six pictures shipped south of the border.[10]

In addition to these direct propaganda functions, both the Office of Inter-American Affairs and the Hays Office provided technical assistance whenever necessary, and applied pressure if studios depicted Latins in an unfavorable light. For example, Whitney convinced Twentieth Century-Fox to spend $40,000 in order to reshoot scenes from *Down Argentine Way* which erroneously described native customs.[11] Whitney's office also encouraged Hollywood stars to travel to Latin America in order to spread good-will and reassert the government's commitment to hemispheric unity. In the first flush of enthusiasm Alice Faye, Wallace

Beery, and Ann Sheridan announced their intention to visit South America, but Whitney scrapped these plans after a Douglas Fairbanks junket proved a disaster. The star inadvertently offended everyone he met.[12]

Thus, the onus of the production of films promoting inter-American unity lay on Hollywood's doorstep. The response of the studio executives was indeed surprising, as the seven major film companies were in the midst of a government-initiated antitrust suit which sought to prevent "block booking" and "blind selling." These sales methods forced theater owners to purchase films in groups from the distributors without any knowledge of the relative merits of the films or the ability to reject any film in the package.[13] Despite the resentment over the government's suit, Hollywood fervently responded to the patriotic call and produced Latin-themed musicals and dramas in record numbers.[14]

Patriotic motives were not the only ones behind the studios' interest in films concerning Latin America. To a certain extent, this wave of Latin films was also a response to the new popularity of South American music and dances. Arthur Freed, mentor of M-G-M musicals, expressed the desire to produce *In Gay Havana* (uncompleted) and explained:

> I believe that hemispheric solidarity, good neighborliness, and the like is only a background reason for the flood of South American features. . . . The actual reason is South American music. . . . Swing music which has held the center stage for five to six years is now passing out and the rhumba stuff is jumping into the number one position in the American taste.[15]

Despite Hollywood's willingness to follow such popular trends, a basic economic rationale can be discerned for the production of films with Latin themes. The coming of the war in Europe drastically lessened the influx of foreign film revenues. Certain countries conquered by the Germans banned American films outright. Others, such as Britain and Australia, needed foreign exchange so desperately that they decreed a 50 percent reduction in the amount spent for American films.[16] By 1940 only Central and South America remained as major importers of American films due to the changing political situation. In order to compensate for lost foreign revenues, Hollywood began to look toward Latin America for economic relief and actively sought this budding market's share of the film dollar. Thus, the film capital's Good Neighbor Policy reflected more than a patriotic gesture in response to government pressure.

Hollywood's attitude toward the Latin countries suddenly bordered on reverence. *Juarez*, the first film of the South American cycle, offered a panegyric to a nineteenth century Mexican president and portrayed him as an equal of Abraham Lincoln.

The shadow of Lincoln haunted this enterprise. Juarez, portrayed by Paul Muni, rarely appeared in his office without a portrait of the Great Emancipator peering over his shoulder. Forced to flee before advancing French troops, Juarez removed his portrait of Lincoln from his office before gathering any of his official documents, thus revealing the importance of the American president to him.

This dramatic link between Juarez and Lincoln leads to the suspicion that Juarez is more of a symbol than a man. The film's rhetoric enforces this interpretation, as the Mexican president's dialogue transcends the historical and borders on the universal. Juarez becomes the "defender of democratic principles," and Maximilian and Napoleon III represent "the dictators who seize power illegally." Juarez's critique of European imperialism suggests an analogy with the United States in the years prior to World War II.

The Mexican president's climactic speech could just as easily have been delivered in Washington, D. C., in 1939 as in Mexico City in 1864:

> By what right, señores, do the Great Powers of Europe invade the lands of simple people . . . kill all who do not make them welcome . . . destroy their fields . . . and take the fruit of their toil from those who survive? . . . The world must know the fate of any usurper who sets his foot upon this soil.[17]

The "political parallels were so closely drawn" that one critic commented that it was not at all difficult to "read between the lines."[18]

Although *Juarez* masked an attempt to urge United States participation in the European war, the film avoided blatant stereotypes of the Mexican and revealed a new found sensitivity towards Latin characters. Juarez was the first "Mexican" hero of the American screen, and Warners assured that he would be portrayed as accurately as possible. Aeneas MacKenzie, one of the film's three screenwriters, left for Mexico City ten months before the initial preparation of the script, although it would have been easy to prepare a scenario from Bertita Harding's *The Phantom Crown* (1934) which Warners had just purchased. During his lengthy visit, MacKenzie read more than seven hundred secondary sources, the President's private and official correspondence, and contemporary newspapers. A portion of the film's dialogue was derived from congressional debates of the period.[19]

Juarez impressed its intended audience both in the United States and Mexico. President Lázaro Cárdenas urged that the film be presented in the Palace of Fine Arts, the first motion picture so honored. The premiere audience responded warmly to the film's message, and stopped the show with applause when Muni explained the difference between constitutional democracy and despotism.[20] The democratic sentiments of *Juarez* were so forcefully expressed that the film became a success in unexpected locales. *Variety* noted that the film did "big biz in India due mainly to its democracy theme and its stress on rule by the people."[21]

With this new found reverence towards the Latin, Hollywood abruptly reversed old stereotypes. No longer was the Latin considered as an ignorant peasant. In RKO's musical comedy *They Met in Argentina* (1941), co-star Buddy Ebsen is surprised as everyone from secretaries to ranchhands are able to speak English with only the slightest trace of an accent. Similarly, films began to portray each nation differently, each possessing an individual culture and history. Again Buddy Ebsen is surprised to learn that Argentine immigration patterns in the nineteenth century paralleled those of the United States. In this manner a lengthy historical discourse becomes *de rigueur* in order to explain the complicated derivation of the name of the *hacendado* Don Enrique de los Santos O'Shea.

Uniting these new images of the Latin was the common assumption that North America and South America were quite similar. For example, the gauchos of *They Met in Argentina* sing the same song that the North American hero sang as a youth on his Texas ranch. The similarity between the two cultures was stressed in order to accentuate the importance of Pan-American unity. The message was often painfully obvious. A critic for *Time* magazine reviewed the finale from Twentieth Century-Fox's *Springtime in the Rockies* (1940) and caustically commented:

The "Pan-American Jubilee" number attempts to be just that by whipping together: 1. Latin America (Cesar Romero, Carmen Miranda and her band), 2. the United States (Betty Grable, John Payne, Harry James and his band), and 3. Canada (large Technicolor chunks of Lake Louise where the action takes place). Only the addition of an Eskimo and a penguin could have made the show still more hemispheric in scope.[22]

Despite Hollywood's apparent good intentions, film-makers actually succeeded in replacing one film stereotype with another. Due to the popularity of the new Latin rhythms—the conga, the samba, the rhumba—Latins became identified with their music, and would rarely appear in American musicals without singing the melodies of their native country. These hip-swaying dances, so different from the sedate North American rhythms, gave Latin artists an increased sensuality which they emphasized in their screen performances.

Yet, this new sensuality, an erotic compensation for years of Latin docility on the screen, rarely achieved its desired fulfillment. Despite the aura of the Latin Lover, the performers from South America rarely managed to marry the hero or heroine. In the 1933 film *Flying Down to Rio* the North American bandleader easily steals Dolores Del Rio from the arms of her "Brazilian" fiancé, Raul Roulien. Nothing has changed by 1941, as James Ellison easily woos Maureen O'Hara, playing an Argentine, away from her boyfriend Alberto Vila in *They Met in Argentina*. The same pattern can be seen in *Too Many Girls* (1940) and *Pan-Americana* (1945), both from RKO studios. Thus, the North American still maintained a sexual superiority over the South American despite a startling reversal in the Latin image in film.

Perhaps the favorite symbol of Latin sensuality was Carmen Miranda, who best represented the extravagant catering to Latin American audiences during the war years. She differed from every movie musical star that Hollywood had yet discovered. Her costume was a combination of native

Bahian dress and a designer's nightmare. With bare legs and midriff, she wore sweeping half-open skirts and tons of colorful costume jewelry. She introduced the turban to the American scene, and topped it with the fruits of her native Brazil. This exaggerated Latin spectacle appeared atop five inch platform shoes, which she claimed to have invented herself. "They come about because I like big men," the five-foot-two-inch star explained. "When I dance with big men I can't see over their shoulders. Maybe they flirt with other girl. So I tell shoemaker to build up my shoes."

Carmen Miranda, born Maria Do Carmo da Cunha, was born in Lisbon and moved to Rio de Janeiro, Brazil, when she was three months old. After finishing her studies in a convent school, she worked in a department store as a model and creator of hats. Actually, she spent more time singing for the other models than engaging in store business.

A guitarist, Josue de Barros, accidentally overheard her singing at the store and arranged her first job on radio. She chose a new name, Carmen Miranda, because her father, a wealthy importer, believed entertainers were vile creatures of the lowest social status. Carmen recalled: "My father used to buy my discs and not know they were mine. He would say to me, 'You know, this Carmen Miranda, she's very good. Everybody talks about her.' I used to sit so quietly and say, 'Yes, Papa,' and inside I would die."

Finally, she was determined to tell her parents. "And, oooh, it was like fireworks. I had a big fight with my father, the neighbors would not look at me, and my boyfriend wanted his ring back. O.K., so I returned the ring, and I snubbed the neighbors. But with my father it turned out fine. I showed him I was a lady."[23]

Lee Shubert discovered her in a Rio nightclub and brought her to Broadway for the "World's Fair" musical,

Streets of Paris (1939). She ignored the title and sang "Sous Samerican Why" ("South American Way") and electrified Broadway audiences. One critic wrote of her premiere: "Her face is too heavy to be beautiful, her figure is nothing to write home about, and she sings in a foreign language. Yet she is the biggest theatrical sensation of the year."

Twentieth Century-Fox brought her to Hollywood and almost singlehandedly Miranda spawned the studio's South American cycle *(Down Argentine Way, Weekend in Havana, That Night in Rio, The Gang's All Here)*. When she arrived in Hollywood, she rented a group of three houses in Beverly Hills. She, her mother, two sisters, and two brothers lived in one; the six Brazilian band members lived in the second; and "some people I feel sorree for" lived in the third. In Hollywood, her home became known as the "second Brazilian embassy." Octavio Tavora, Brazilian Consulate attache in Hollywood, noted, "Everybody who came from Brazil wanted to visit her. Carmen was the Mary Pickford of Hollywood. She was in everybody's heart."

After each film her popularity grew, and she performed more and was given more songs and dialogue. Fox studios supposedly encouraged her to learn English on a fiscal basis. They promised her fifty cents for each bona fide and usable word that she added to her vocabulary. By the end of her first summer, Miranda acquired four hundred new words and a raise in salary of two hundred dollars. Despite this profitable method of learning English, Miranda's manhandling of the language won her countless admirers. She explained, "I know p'raps one hondred words—pretty good for Sous American girl, no? Best I know ten English words: *men, men, men, men,* and *monee, monee, monee, monee, monee, monee.*"

Mack Gordon and Harry Warren became her official composers. Although supervised by Gilberto Souto, who supplied Portuguese translations for Miranda, Gordon and

Warren provided the inspiration for the songs of Fox's
South American cycle. Gordon vouched for the authentic-
ity of his songs. After *Weekend in Havana,* he explained, "I
feel confident of turning out a good job—I've been smoking
Havana cigars for fifteen years!" He received similar inspiration for other Miranda films: "When we wrote the songs
for *That Night in Rio,* we went to Monterey and took an isolated cottage on the bay there. You see, Rio is also on a
bay."[24]

Her most fondly remembered film, *The Gang's All Here*
(1943), combined the talents of the queen of comic excess
with the king—Busby Berkeley—and produced a bizarre
display of inter-American unity. The film opens on a half-
lit floating face, reminiscent of the "Lullaby of Broadway"
number from *Gold Diggers of 1935.* Suddenly, the camera
shifts to a nightclub stage where a model of the *S. S. Brazil*
is docking and unloading the major products of its country:
coffee, bananas, strawberries, and then Carmen Miranda.
Her hat, naturally, contains Brazil's chief exports. The
night club host, Phil Baker, proclaims: "Well, there's your
Good Neighbor Policy!" Miranda responds by teaching everyone the "Uncle Sam-ba," a dance containing elements
of both North and South American rhythms.

The rest of the film, a standard love plot with Alice Faye
and James Ellison, pales in comparison with Miranda's big
number, the exotic "Girl in the Tutti-Frutti Hat." Carmen
Miranda, drawn on a cart driven by golden oxen, arrives
on a desert island laden with palm trees. The island's natives, beautiful women with six-foot bananas as hats, begin
their dance. Others, carrying strawberries between their
legs, lie on the floor in a typical Busby Berkeley star formation. The bananas then descend into the strawberries'
midst in a sensuous slow motion rape. The banana laden
natives eventually fall asleep, and Carmen Miranda leaves
the stage of the most erotic production number of the

1940s. Ironically, this scene was snipped by censors in Miranda's native Brazil.[25]

The popularity of these films with Latin locales, plots, and music pleasantly surprised studio executives. *Down Argentine Way,* the first film of the Latin musical cycle, did "sensational business in New York, and gave the State Theater one of its biggest Saturday grosses ever." The *Variety* critic expressed his enthusiasm, noting that "the picture's reception in Latin America would provide studios with an angle on the potentialities of upping income on big pictures with backgrounds of those countries instead of European settings." He then confidently prophesied that this picture would "inspire a new cycle of films in the Amazon, pampas, and Andes regions."[26]

This analysis revealed a common assumption, namely, that the Latin orientation of the plot, locale, or music would be sure to please Latin audiences. In this manner Hollywood continually underestimated Latin audiences by assuming that they could only understand what was familiar to them. For example, when Bud Abbott and Lou Costello appeared in *In the Navy* (1941), officials of the Whitney office and Hollywood screenwriters recommended that special title cards be added in order to explain the jokes to South American audiences. A Universal studio executive explained that "Latins have a different sense of humor than film audiences in the United States." He added: "They take their pictures seriously. If they see a little fat guy poke the admiral in the rear with a sixteen inch gun, they will get the idea that the navy is made up of virtually nothing but little fat guys tickling their officers with heavy artillery."[27] In a like manner producers reasoned that Latin-oriented films would be easily understandable to South American audiences and consequently of great popularity.

Hollywood's pretensions of inter-American good will hardly prepared studio officials for the acerbic response of

Latin American critics and audiences since the warm reception for *Juarez* had lulled them into a sense of security.
Local representatives of the film companies noted that
goodwill gestures might be turning sour when *Argentine
Nights* with the Ritz Brothers and the Andrews Sisters was
"hooted off the screen" and almost caused a riot in an Argentine theatre.[28] *Down Argentine Way* brought similar
complaints: why was Carmen Miranda portraying an Argentine when she was obviously a Brazilian? Why were Ar-
gentines depicted as the owners of a crooked race track and
the Americans once again as the good guys?[29]

Latin Americans possessed a double resentment against
these films. First, they were annoyed by the misinterpreta-
tions of their culture which occurred frequently despite
the plethora of technical advisers available to screenwriters. Brazilians were among the most sensitive, resenting
any intimation that their nation possessed a substantial In-
dian population.[30] Even if films ignored this aspect of Latin
society, they still had a tendency to show "South American
characters in tight-laced pants and long sideburns or
shawls and mantillas." "That's museum stuff," sneered one
film director.[31]

Secondly, Latin American critics resented the inter-
American unity message which was clearly evident in each
film. *Sintonia,* an Argentine weekly, argued that the
"United States goodwill drive, via films, radio, and the
press has taken on the characteristics of a spiritual blitz-
krieg prepared in the arsenals of Yankee advertising." Additionally, local filmmakers argued that "this Good Neighbor Policy might become dangerous to us although the
United States wishes us no harm." They reasoned that the
"Yanqui cine" was "striking a blow" at the nascent Argentine film industry, by crowding local productions out of the
marketplace since local audiences preferred the more pro-
fessionally made American films.[32]

Despite Latin criticism from the very beginning of the South American musical cycle, Hollywood continued with these domestically popular films. Although Whitney scrapped his proposed series of Latin American junkets after Douglas Fairbank's disastrous visit, he still expressed his intention of "pushing ahead with the plan for hypoing American solidarity via films, despite the conviction in some South American quarters that the whole idea should be dropped."[33]

The end of the war did more to dampen Hollywood's enthusiasm with Latin films than did complaints from South America. After the liberation previously closed markets once again received American films. Business abroad in the three months following the end of the war exceeded grosses of the entire year preceding Pearl Harbor. Audiences in France, Belgium, and the Philippines flocked to theatres in unprecedented numbers in order to escape a war-weary world.[34] This ended Hollywood's brief dependence on Latin markets.

Adding to the decline in films with Latin themes after the war was the increased influence of dubbing. Metro-Goldwyn-Mayer began with *Gaslight* in 1944 and dubbed all future films with Spanish speaking New York actors. Paramount swiftly followed with *The Song of Bernadette*, and the results were surprising. Second-rate dubbed films managed to outgross titled classics. Sam Berger, Loew's regional director for Latin America, noted that dubbing had led to a fifty to ninety percent increase in business, as dubbed versions of *Gaslight* and *Bathing Beauty* outgrossed a subtitled *Gone With the Wind.*[35] Chile remained the only exception to this trend, since Chileans, with their strong regional Spanish accent, found it difficult to understand films dubbed by American Spanish speaking actors.[36]

The public was also tiring of the barrage of Latin American films. It is not surprising that two post-war Broadway musicals presented songs dealing with the weariness with South American music. In *Call Me Mister* (1946) Betty Garrett sang "South America, Take It Away," urging the Latins to "take back the rhumba, mambo, and samba" because "her back was aching from all that shaking." Noel Coward also presented a weary "Nina" *(Sigh No More)*, who was tired of "beginning the Beguine" and needed a lengthy rest. This fatigued young woman also considered "Carmen Miran-da, subversive propagan-da."

Despite Hollywood's sudden lack of interest in Latin America after the war's end, the film version of the Good Neighbor Policy had beneficial and unexpected results. It reversed a thirty-year-old Latin stereotype of the violent, dirty, and lazy South American and presented a continent with educated classes and indigenous tribes with a valid culture. While Latins still rarely married North Americans in films of this period, they fraternized freely and openly. By the end of the war, the Latin had become a familiar film fixture, portrayed as basically equal to white Yankees and only slightly different in culture.

The magnitude of this quantum leap in stereotypes pardons Hollywood's occasional excesses in the realm of the Latin American musical. While blacks and other domestic minority groups remained pariahs on film, the Latins suddenly became the "Good Neighbors" next door. Although Latin stereotypes have not been entirely eliminated from the screen, Hollywood's forced sensitivity of the World War II era has made this elusive goal somewhat closer.

10

Separate But Equal:
Blacks in Wartime Musicals

The democratic musical embraced all races and creeds. Latin Americans, former outcasts of this mythical world, suddenly began to mix freely with their neighbors to the North. While men on the homefront felt free to court Latin women as Dennis Morgan did in the "Good Night, Good Neighbor" sequence of *Thank Your Lucky Stars,* Latin men also appeared to help the war effort. Soldiers named López or Gutiérrez suddenly began to associate with the Smiths and the Joneses.

Although the musical welcomed the Latin with open arms, it maintained a curious ambivalence towards a domestic minority group. The musical melting pot presented blacks with only a half-hearted enthusiasm. The "separate but equal" dictum which governed black life in the society as a whole became the tacit rule governing the black's entrance into the world of the musical. As a result, blacks were as segregated on the screen as in real life.

The performances of black entertainers in the star-studded revues of the wartime period remained rigidly separated from the rest of the film and the white actors and actresses. Their numbers habitually began and ended with an audience applauding or a curtain rising or falling. These stock shots bracketed the performance and isolated it from the rest of the film. Part of the logic of this move was the feeling that Southern censors would be able to snip scenes with black performers with little difficulty. In this fashion, the Lena Horne performance in *Thousands Cheer* or *Ziegfeld Follies* would never be missed even by observant audiences.

The irony of these segregated musical numbers was the fact that the songs black actors were required to sing often reinforced the image of racial democracy that the musicals were trying to maintain. For example, midway through *Hollywood Canteen*, the Golden Gate Quartet appears out of nowhere to sing "The General Jumped at Dawn." This song explains that "white men and black men" form an "All-American team" which would help the United States to win the war:

> The general had a groovy crew
> A million lads and I'm telling you
> There were white men, black men, on the beam,
> A real solid All-American team.
> He had tall men, small men, fat and lean
> The fighting-est crew that you've ever seen.
> Every creed and color and every belief,
> From an eskimo to an Indian chief.*

As the lyrics count the many races and religions that participate in the battle, the camera pans from face to face in the soldier audience. Each face depicts the appropriate ethnic, religious, or racial group. These soldiers formerly composed a faceless mass which crowded the Hollywood Can-

---

*"The General Jumped at Dawn," by James Mundy. © 1943 by Bregman, Vocco & Conn, Inc. Copyright renewed 1970. All rights reserved. Used by permission.

teen. Only in this song do the many soldiers appear as individuals. As the Golden Gate Quartet sings its last note, the various races and creeds seemingly disappear and are not seen again during the film.

Thank Your Lucky Stars, the other Warner Brothers all-star cavalcade of the period, also presents a black mini-musical. The curtain rises at a charity benefit to reveal Hattie McDaniels and Willie Best performing "Ice Cold Katie" with a large chorus of black singers and dancers. Willie Best, the shuffling janitor in Warner's *Juke Girl* only the year before, is suddenly elevated to the role of soldier. Miss Katie Brown (McDaniels) refuses to do her "patriotic duty" and "marry the soldier" who is "soon going off to war." Katie relents after the continual appeals of the chorus and finally decides to marry Private Jones (Best). However, it is almost too late. After the "I Do's," Best must return to his army unit before it is shipped overseas.

In a manner of speaking, the "Ice Cold Katie" number is quite an advance. McDaniel and Best are no longer maid and butler, but woman and soldier, separated by the coming of war, a dilemma common to both whites and blacks. Yet, the curtain descends immediately after the song ends, and *Thank Your Lucky Stars* returns to the problems of its white protagonists.

In *Holiday Inn,* when Bing Crosby sings his praise of the Great Emancipator in "Abraham," Louise Beavers joins him in song but remains in the distant kitchen as the camera cuts from room to room. Bing is even unaware that his maid is singing, even though the melody is ostensibly a duet. *Sun Valley Serenade* is almost as remarkable. Glenn Miller and the Band play "Chattanooga Choo-Choo," and suddenly, out of nowhere, the fantastic Nicholas Brothers appear. This limberlegged duo performs its number before a cartoon-like backdrop of the "Choo-Choo," and then as the music finishes they abruptly disappear. Who were they? The audience has no idea, as the segment is completely segregated from the rest of the film. Miller continues playing, taking no notice of the mysteriously vanishing blacks.

Perhaps the most interesting case of racial separation occurred in *You'll Never Get Rich* when reluctant draftee Fred Astaire is tossed into jail with several black enlisted men. Although publicity stills show Fred and the soldiers singing together, the film itself is markedly different. Confined in a jail cell, Fred and his cohorts are never shown together in the same shot. Fred dances throughout the cell, while the camera cuts to the corner of the cell where the blacks are playing their instruments. The only link between the two shots is an omnipresent trumpet which protrudes from the corner of the screen. The audience thus *assumes* a black soldier is accompanying Fred's dance. In some release prints, their joint presence is never shown on the screen. By clever cutting, blacks were once again eliminated from the film without damaging the continuity.

Hollywood made no concession to calls for integration in its musicals which featured both white and black performers. However, the creators of the musical comedy solved this paradox of race segregation in a supposedly democratic society by providing two all-black musicals, *Cabin in the Sky* (1943) and *Stormy Weather* (1944). Each film epitomized the "separate but equal" doctrine which governed race relations in wartime society. In this way, blacks were given musicals which adopted all the conventions of the "white" musicals, but at no time were white performers present in these films. The musicals thus approached a segregationist ideal.

The appearance of these all-black musicals within a year's time was not coincidence. The *New York Times* stated that both Metro-Goldwyn-Mayer and Twentieth Century-Fox were "following the desires of Washington in making such films at this time. Decisions to produce the pictures followed official expression that the Administration felt that its program for increased employment of Negro citizens in certain heretofore restricted fields of industry would be helped by a general distribution of important pictures in which Negroes played a major part."[1] These films would have a propaganda value as they seemingly demonstrated that America did not discriminate against its black citizens as the Nazis often maintained.

Cabin in the Sky attempted to view blacks as representative of all races and creeds, but it failed to produce anything but a musical *Green Pastures*. Even the title cards noted that "the folklore of America has its origins in all lands, all races, and all colors." Yet the blacks of *Cabin in the Sky* remained trapped in a mythical world of angels and devils, wholly apart from the everyday reality of wartime society.

This was Vincente Minnelli's second film for M-G-M, and he performed a creditable job of adapting the Vernon Duke and John LaTouche Broadway musical. *Cabin in the Sky* gathered all the black talent available to M-G-M: Ethel Waters, Lena Horne, Eddie "Rochester" Anderson, Rex Ingram, Mantan Moreland, Butterfly McQueen, and the Duke Ellington Orchestra. Even Louis Armstrong appeared in a minor role as the devil's assistant. New songs by Harold Arlen and E.Y. Harburg, which have since become classic ("Happiness Is a Thing Called Joe"), were added to the already rich score.

Despite this considerable array of talent, many critics despised the film. Manny Farber lamented that *Cabin in the Sky* constructed a "niggertown," and felt that "there would be no movie made about the Negro until one is made about him in relation to the rest of the country of which he composes ten percent. His blues, dress, his whole attitude, do not exist in a vacuum, but have meaning only as they are seen inside the society that made them."[2] Thus, both contemporary and modern audiences maintain a curious ambivalence about the film, since they are impressed by the brilliant performances but are offended by Hollywood's simplistic and romanticized version of black life in the South.

The protagonists of *Cabin in the Sky* are either profoundly religious or depraved gamblers, prostitutes, or murderers. There is no middle ground in the portrait of black life presented in this film. The blacks become merely cardboard representations of the lifelong struggle between good and evil, which the characters of *Cabin in the Sky* symbolize and represent.

As the film opens, all of the blacks in this southern town are arriving at church. Missing only are Petunia (Ethel Waters) and Little Joe (Eddie Anderson). The preacher goes to seek them out, and discovers that Petunia has persuaded Little Joe to give up gambling and follow the path of the Lord. Petunia drags her recalcitrant husband to church, as the Hall Johnson Choir sings "Li'l Black Sheep" ("Li'l black sheep, come home once more; Shepherd towed him through the door"). Joe's friends lure him away from the service for one last crap game. Soon afterwards, a shot is heard, and Petunia discovers her Joe dying on the floor of a local night club. Domino Johnson, an ex-con, shot Joe for using loaded dice.

As Joe teeters on the brink of death, Petunia, the firm believer, prays for his soul. The devil appears to take Joe away, but God's messengers, summoned by Petunia's pleas, also arrive and begin negotiations for the body. The divine representatives decide to give Joe six months to reform, but there is one slight catch. He will have no memory of this arrangement when he returns to life. If he does not "whitewash his soul" in this period, then the devil may have him. Joe's soul becomes an other-worldly prize, as both the forces of Good and Evil try to win him over.

Joe returns to life, and for the time being gives up his shiftless, no-account ways. Lucifer, Jr., tempts poor Joe with the fancies of Miss Georgia Brown (Lena Horne) and a winning sweepstakes ticket. Joe resists, but Petunia accidently sees him and Georgia embracing, and she kicks her husband out of the house. Joe, saddened by losing Petunia, returns to his former dissolute life, living high and frequenting the gambling tables at Jim Hendry's nightclub.

Petunia realizes her error and makes one last attempt to save her Joe before the six months expire. She goes to Joe's favorite night spot, dressed in a fancy gold lame dress, and tries to make Joe jealous by flirting with Domino Johnson. Joe repents and punches Domino in an attempt to win back Petunia's love. Domino draws a gun as Petunia prays to God to destroy this wicked place.

Suddenly, the M-G-M tornado, languishing on a backlot since *The Wizard of Oz,* reappears and destroys the nightclub. But, it is too late, as both Joe and Petunia are killed by Domino. They awake in heavenly robes, and, after Petunia's prayers, they are both permitted to enter St. Peter's Gate. As the screen blurs into a cloudy heaven, Little Joe wakes from his delirium. This has all been a dream. Naturally, Joe has learned from his evil ways and decides to take the path of the Lord. Petunia is thrilled, and the film ends as she sings "Happiness Is a Thing Called Joe."

The blacks of *Cabin in the Sky* are extremely superstitious, believing in angels and devils in the context of their strong religious fervor. Ethel Waters' majestic presence makes her love for Little Joe believable, but the rest of the film suffers from racial stereotypes all too prevalent in Hollywood films. The second all-black musical of the wartime period avoided these mythical conceptions of black life, and, as a result, presented a contemporary view of blacks in *Stormy*

Weather (1943). Although once again an all-black, or "segregated," musical, this Andrew Stone film placed blacks on the same Great White Way that Caucasians had always travelled in *Tin Pan Alley, The Great Ziegfeld,* or *Broadway Melody of 1940.*

Stormy Weather unintentionally parodied all of the Twentieth Century-Fox musicals, and, as a result, appeared almost a white musical in blackface. Like many of the Fox films, *Stormy Weather* concerns the life and loves of a musical star, the famous black dancer, "Bill Williamson" (Bill Robinson). In this case the biography is wholly imaginary, merely the excuse for a panoramic vista of black music and entertainers from World War I to the present. Like *Alexander's Ragtime Band* (1938), *Stormy Weather* adopts the "cavalcade approach" to its music. While the former presented melodies from Irving Berlin shows, the latter searches for black roots in the *Blackbirds* revues of the late 1920s and early 1930s and the songs of Fats Waller and other black artists.

Aside from the different tempos of music, the film follows the standard Fox pattern. The mail arrives at Bill Williamson's home, and neighborhood children discover that *Theatre World Magazine* has designated him as a "credit to his race." The congratulatory advertisements from Bill's friends trigger memories and provide the appropriate flashbacks which give the film its structure. Bill first recalls the return of his "all-Negro unit" from World War I. This follows the wartime trend of depicting blacks as full-fledged soldiers in the fight for democracy.

Bill meets Selina Rogers (Lena Horne) in a black nightclub. She is a famous singer, and, when she sees Bill dance, she encourages him to "study and work hard so he can become successful." "Ambition" is her key to celebrity status. In this fashion, the white success myth is transferred to these black performers.

Even the musical numbers strive to conform to white norms. At first, as Bill struggles his way upward in second-rate shows and night clubs, the musical numbers (staged by Clarence Robinson) attempt to maintain a certain black character. Unfortunately, these numbers provide a racist parody of the black image in the American mind. Here the African native beating his tom-tom becomes the symbol of black music. The women dress in zebra skins and ostrich feathers. A cakewalk number is even worse, as the chorus members don large hats with smiling sambo faces on top.

However, once Bill achieves success, this stereotypical motif disappears. As Bill and Lena sing "I Can't Give You Anything But Love, Baby," the whole atmosphere changes. The white stage features ionic columns, luxurious chandeliers, and a long stairway. Men in tuxedos await the entry of Lena on the stairway in an eerie foreshadowing of the "Hello Dolly" number of some twenty-five years later. Then, suddenly, Bill and Lena begin dancing on a floor of mirrors. Is this *Stormy Weather* or Fred Astaire and Eleanor Powell's "Begin the Beguine" in *Broadway Melody of 1940?*

Bill wants to settle down, but Lena wishes to continue performing. They separate for a few years, until Cab Calloway slyly manages to bring them together at a benefit for black soldiers going overseas. Cab's appearance and the performance of "Jumpin' Jive" is no surprise. Kay Kyser, Benny Goodman, Glenn Miller, Paul Whiteman, and the other big band leaders regularly appeared in the wartime musicals, often performing key roles in the film's plot. Cab Calloway provides a black equivalent of this trend.

Bill and Lena unite in song. Cab sings "Ain't That Something to Shout About," and the film ends with the lovers happily reunited as in the other Fox musicals. The producers of the film were proud of the results and pleased by their avoidance of common racial stereotypes:

Producer William LeBaron explained how one line of dialogue was eventually cut. When a character was asked
where he got his new suit, his reply had been, "I won it in
a crap game."[3]

While, in certain respects, the film avoided standard
black stereotypes, it perpetuated others. The "natural sense
of rhythm" myth pervades the film. No black is able to keep
still once the music starts. Bill is dead tired after swabbing
the deck for ten hours. He lies down, but suddenly hears
a harmonica. Immediately, his feet begin tapping, and he
joins the jam session. The black audience in the film's
nightclub sequences is similarly unable to control itself.
While white audiences in *The Gang's All Here*, made in the
same year, applaud politely, the blacks clap in rhythm,
swing and sway to the music, and often jump on the tables
to dance. Thus, when Lena explains that "singing is in my
blood," it is more than a metaphor.

11

Democracy in Action

The musical melting pot idealized American democracy for its ability to eliminate racial and ethnic discrimination. Blacks, Latins, Irish, Italians, and Chinese all participated in this musical society on an equal basis. Film musicals also exalted a second facet of the unique American experience— the eradication of class differences in a society dominated by neither rich or poor.

Comedies, dramas, and musical films of the wartime period all glossed over the question of class divisions in American society and almost pretended that they were nonexistent. For example, *The Devil and Miss Jones* (1941) presented the most charming millionaire of the wartime era. At first, Charles Coburn portrays a crotchety department store magnate who attempts to infiltrate a labor organization in one of his stores. While disguised as a shoe salesman, he discovers the wondrous charms of the working classes. A weekend at Coney Island, a bottle of beer, and cheese sandwiches were the simple pleasures that millionaires could never hope to enjoy. Coburn solves his dilemma by giving the workers all they desire and marrying the kindly Spring Byington of the shoe department. The problem of millionaires is their lack of understanding. If they could discover the true virtues and problems of the American worker, all labor problems and class divisions would disappear.

The Hollywood musical followed this trend as it sought to eliminate class tensions in the films of wartime. *Higher and Higher* (RKO, 1943) purported to be an adaptation of the Rodgers and Hart stage musical of 1940. However, the young Frank Sinatra arrived, and the original script and score were revamped in order to showcase the talents of this youthful sensation. All that remained of the original score was a curious song entitled "Disgustingly Rich":

> I'll buy everything I wear at Saks
> I'll cheat plenty on my income tax.
> Swear like a trooper,
> Live in a stupor,
> Just disgustingly rich.*

The message of *Higher and Higher* is that the values of the rich are outdated. The future of American society lies in cooperation. Mr. Drake (Leon Errol), a former millionaire, is in dire straits. His home is about to be repossessed by the bank. He needs help, but his wealthy friends refuse. His true allies are his maid, butler, valet, and cook. Drake, unlike most of the wealthy, has treated his servants as equals. They eat at the same table with him, they converse as friends. At first the servants attempt to play the game of the rich. They disguise Millie the kitchen maid as Mr. Drake's daughter, and attempt to marry her to the suave and wealthy aristocrat Victor Borge in the hope of saving the Drake household. The scheme flops as the Count is revealed as a penniless fraud. The only hope for the servants becomes hard work. They convert the basement of the Drake home into a tavern. It becomes exceedingly popular

---

and the house is saved. Thus, cooperation between rich and poor solves the problem, not the vain attempt to imitate false and corrupt manners of wealthy society.

Higher and Higher admits that a useless leisure class exists in American society. In *The Gang's All Here,* also released in 1943, the rich become active supporters of the American war effort and a truly admired segment of American society. Edward Everett Horton decides to present the cast of the Club New Yorker in a show at his upcoming garden party. The admission to the performance would be paid in war bonds. Phil Baker, the Club's manager, hears this news and says to Horton: "You remind me of my two favorite people—Santa Claus and Uncle Sam," because he is both generous and patriotic.

Charlotte Greenwood, Horton's wife, first appears as the upper class snob. Within minutes, however, she cuts loose in the wild high-kicking dance for which she is justly famous, and reveals that she is a former showgirl. There are no class barriers here, and marriage into a wealthy family seems wholly unproblematical. Similarly, no fuss is made when the daughter runs off with the Spanish dancer Tony De Marco.

This is quite a change from the musicals of the 1930s. Consider Rodgers and Hart's *Hot Heiress,* where Ona Munson, a rich young woman, falls in love with a riveter who is working on a skyscraper opposite her apartment building. She brings him to the family estate where everyone takes considerable delight in embarrassing this man of humble origins. The young lovers eventually marry, but only after the entire family is alienated.

Faceless millionaires and industrial barons hardly provided the main problem for the democratic orientation of these musical films. Of far more importance were yet another social group: the Hollywood stars. Both rich and famous, the stars caused the American public to wonder what they were doing for the war effort. Although several Hollywood stars actually enlisted in the armed forces, it still appeared as though the life of the Hollywood star continued as usual.

Yet, film magazines attempted to portray the musical stars as no different from every American citizen: "Like thousands of her countrywomen, Jeanette MacDonald has waved her soldier goodby. With the mixed emotions so many of us have known and are to know, she stood at the rail of an airport and watched his ship take off—hoping, dreading, proud of him, heavy with the foretaste of loneliness, and above all, strong in the knowledge that his going was not only inevitable, but right."[1]

Yet, for every Gene Raymond, there appeared to be an Errol Flynn, flashing a toothy smile across the nation and impregnating every young woman in sight. What indeed were Hollywood stars doing for the war effort? Judy Garland may be planting a victory garden, as *Photoplay* announced, but fans wondered if this was sacrifice enough. Could the stars do more?

On an individual level, little of lasting importance could be achieved. Judy Garland and Vincente Minnelli once invited a lone soldier up to their hotel suite for coffee and cake. They sat at the piano and sang until four in the morning. The soldier then decided to go and thanked them for a good time. Minnelli took him to the elevator, and asked, "You know who that was singing for you?"

"All I know is that she's a lovely girl," answered the soldier.

"That was Judy Garland," said Minnelli.

"My goodness! She's my favorite actress," exclaimed the soldier. "And I didn't even ask her for her autograph. Now when I tell the fellows at camp that I was with Judy Garland, they'll never believe me."[2]

Despite the kindness of this musical duo, the incident

must have seemed an ironic dream to the soldier by the next morning. More than a single night on the town was needed to boost the morale of America's men at war.

The Canteen provided the ideal means for the film star to do his or her bit. Broadway began the trend in early 1942 with the Stage Door Canteen, which opened in the basement of the 44th Street Theatre. Jane Cowl and Selena Royle were the chairwomen of this effort of the American Theatre Wing. They urged stars to participate in both the construction and the staffing of the new canteen. The endeavor was run almost like a Broadway show. Cowl warned that "if volunteers signed up, they would have to work for the duration. If they failed to appear, they were obliged to provide an understudy." The goal was to "provide gratuitous food and entertainment for soldiers and sailors. Snacks sufficient to keep our boys from going hungry would be served by the young pretty girls of the theatre who would be hostesses."[3]

The Stage Door Canteen opened on March 2, 1942, and, according to Brooks Atkinson, *New York Times* critic, "it seemed as if it had been there always."[4] What most surprised viewers was the democratic style represented by the Canteen, as stars and soldiers participated equally in this new endeavor. Carl Van Vechten wrote: "The place is absolutely democratic in its organization and social behavior, perhaps one of the few democratic institutions in existence anywhere: English soldiers, sailors, and RAF men dance beside, mingle, and eat with Chinese airmen, Americans from every branch of the service, including Negroes and Indians, Canadians, Australians, South Africans, Dutch and French sailors (how pleasant it is to listen to the *bon soirs* which greet them from every side of the room when they enter), occasionally Russians: all are a part of the Stage Door Canteen. . . . Is it any wonder that almost everyone who sees the Stage Door Canteen for the first time bursts into tears from sheer happiness that such things can be?"[5] In addition to the camaraderie among the members of the armed forces of various nations of the world, was the surprising friendship of the Broadway actors and actresses who welcomed the soldiers with open arms.

The Hollywood Canteen opened soon afterwards, thanks to the efforts of Bette Davis and John Garfield, and soon became as successful as its New York equivalent. Both Canteens became immortalized soon after their openings in two all-star musical films. Although both *Stage Door Canteen* and *Hollywood Canteen* emphasized the racial and ethnic equality that Carl Van Vechten had found so surprising, the contributions of the stars to the war effort were given precedence. Sol Lesser, the producer of *Stage Door Canteen,* explained this emphasis in an advertisement for the film: "A print of this picture will be placed in a vault in our national capital and in London, so that people a hundred years from now can know a few straight facts about show folks and how they worked and gave of themselves as hostesses, busboys, entertaining on the Canteen stage or otherwise waiting on the soldiers of the United Nations."[6]

Director Frank Borzage's *Stage Door Canteen* demonstrated that stars would give their all to help the American soldier. The film begins as a platoon of soldiers, each named after the state of their birth, arrive in New York. As in most of the soldier films of this period, the boys are given one day to see the Big Apple. Dakota, California, and Jersey visit a posh restaurant for lunch. The waiter tips them off that they can get the same food for free across the street at the Stage Door Canteen.

Dakota and his friends enter the Canteen as Lillian leaves. She is in tears because she has broken the Canteen's cardinal rule—she dated a soldier after hours. Selena Royle fires her and tears up her entry card. As the audience learns, only women with the highest morals may be Canteen girls.

Dakota is astounded to see the stellar talent in the Canteen that night. Ed Wynn checks hats, Alan Mowbray is a busboy, George Raft does the dishes, and Katherine Cornell passes out oranges to the boys. Dakota meets Eileen, a young actress, who has come to the canteen in hope of meeting a Broadway producer. She talks to Dakota but tells him nothing, using the Canteen's rules to fend off his queries: "I'm sorry but girls aren't allowed to tell where they live; I'm sorry but you can't tell me your destination."

As Dakota and Eileen chat, Helen Hayes arrives to dance with the boys. "It would be an honor," she says to the soldiers. The stars at the Canteens always defer to the soldiers. The stars appear humble and appreciative of the tasks that the soldiers are doing, and the aura of the Hollywood or Broadway star is deliberately played down. Tallulah Bankhead furthers this image as she says to California, "You do your job well on your side, and don't forget we'll be doing our job on this side."

Kenny Baker begins to sing "Good Night Sweetheart," the last song of the evening, and all the soldiers leave. Strangely enough, Eileen misses Dakota. She overhears her roommate reading a letter from her soldier brother: "Of course, there's a chance that I may not come back from this war." When Eileen understands that Dakota might also die in battle, she realizes what a heel she had been that night.

Fortunately, the men's passes are extended. Dakota returns to the Canteen to see Eileen. She, in the meantime, has won an acting job opposite Paul Muni: "This is the day I've been waiting for, but somehow I don't have the kick I've expected." After a dinner with Muni, Eileen rushes to the Canteen to meet Dakota. They kiss and resolve to marry. They decide to meet the next night at the Canteen.

Eileen waits outside for Dakota to arrive, since she has lost her membership card for dating a soldier. Katharine Hepburn learns of the situation and allows her to enter since she will be a married woman. Dakota never arrives because his division has been sent overseas. Eileen is heartbroken, but the venerable Kate gives her a pep talk designed to inspire any woman.

"Yes, that's right, we're in a war and we've got to win. And we're going to win. And that's why the boy you love is going overseas. And isn't that maybe why you're going to go back in there and get on your job? Look, you're a good kid and I don't wonder why he loves you. He knows what he's fighting for. He's fighting for the kind of world in which you and he can live together in happiness, in peace, in love. Don't ever think about quitting. Don't ever stop for a minute working, fighting, praying until we've got that kind of a world for you, for him, for your children, for the whole human race for days without end. Amen."

The scene fades as an anonymous announcer proclaims: "Tonight and every night until victory, millions of men will find escape from the miseries of war at the Stage Door Canteen."

The film was a rousing success, especially among soldiers. Attendance at the Canteen reached four thousand men per night after the film was released. The film did more than hype attendance, for, as one Canteen hostess claimed, "Since the Stage Door Canteen picture, the boys are certainly making a pitch for glamour. Some take their cue from the film and start talking in familiar tones about the Lunts and Katherine Cornell and want to know how soon they'll be on."

Another commented: "Remember California, the guy in the picture who's never been kissed. Thanks to the film we're attracting a number of Californias who apparently never before had the courage to enter a Canteen. There's a quiet demeanor and shy reserve about them which lend an added touch of dignity to the place."

One of the administrators agreed with the hostesses' observations: "It's a metamorphosis that's given a whole new tone to the Canteen, in which gentility and a fine pose play a leading role. It's a case of the Hollywood conception of how a soldier boy should act being superimposed on the real thing—with results that are completely to the liking of the hostesses."[7]

Hollywood Canteen presented a similar concept of stellar democracy. Slim (Robert Hutton), a lonely sailor on a South Pacific island, sits in the rain viewing a badly faded print of *The Hard Way* (Warners, 1943). He sees Joan Leslie and immediately falls in love with the budding starlet. Months later Slim's ship docks in California, where he and his friend, Sergeant Nolan (Dane Clark), wander into the Hollywood Canteen. The soldiers gape at Jane Wyman and Barbara Stanwyck, as friends explain the ideal of the Canteen, where "Humphrey Bogart waits on tables and Ann Sheridan makes sandwiches." Sergeant Nolan is impressed: "I used to think that Hollywood was all false fronts. They're not false; they're friendly. Democracy means that everybody is equal—where all those big shots talk to little shots like me."

Slim is the millionth sailor to enter the Canteen, so he is allowed to chose any star as his date for the weekend. Naturally, he chooses Joan Leslie. Joan is the exact opposite of the prototypical Hollywood star. She is shy and modest, "like a person you can go up and say hello to." Joan takes Slim to her home, a modest bungalow where she lives with her parents. Her folks are at the movies, so they cannot go inside since they are unchaperoned. "It wouldn't look right," she explains. The romantic vision of the seductive and loose Hollywood starlet is dramatically reversed in

Leslie's portrayal. She is more the girl next door than the Hollywood pin-up queen.

Slim returns to the Canteen and thanks his hosts: "I may be number one million, but I represent every man in the room. I might have been a Russian friend, a colored boy, or one of our South American neighbors. I'm all of you rolled into one." He leaves quickly since his ship is departing. Joan Leslie meets him at the dock and hints that she will wait for him to return from the front.

The music of the Hollywood Canteen reinforces the film's democratic message. The Andrew Sisters sing the title song, explaining that "G. I. Joes can forget their woes and boogie with any movie star." In another song the Sisters explain that they're "getting corns for their country" by doing "a patriotic jitterbug" while waiting tables at the Canteen.

The Canteen films thus accomplished two purposes. First, they displayed the American racial and ethnic melting pot in action. Secondly, and more importantly, these motion pictures presented the Hollywood star as a regular guy or gal, tormented by the same problems as every American citizen. The films helped to dispel the myth of the Hollywood star as a person set apart from American society as it mobilized for war, for the stars were now perceived as doing their bit for the war effort.

Twentieth Century-Fox continued this trend with a distaff version of the Canteen films. *Four Jills and a Jeep* (1944) told the real life adventures of Kay Francis, Carole Landis, Martha Raye, and Mitzi Mayfair on a five-month army camp tour throughout Europe and North Africa. Director William Seiter admitted that the film tended to glamorize the actual events. It was decided that the four women would be well dressed and well groomed each time they appeared on an army base in the film. Actually, the troupe performed four or five times each day. They rarely wore make-up, their hair was usually disheveled, and they often dressed in bulky sweaters. Even their army plane was spruced up for the film. The aluminum bucket seats were replaced by the upholstered variety.[8]

Kay, Carole, Martha, and Mitzi were not alone in their tour of the front. They were joined by virtually every musical star on the Twentieth lot: Phil Silvers, Dick Haymes, Alice Faye, Betty Grable, Carmen Miranda, and George Jessel. Even Tommy Dorsey and his Orchestra made frequent appearances. Like the Canteen films, *Four Jills and a Jeep* featured a romance between a star (Carole Landis) and a soldier, Ted Warren (John Harvey). However, unlike the fictional romances of Joan Leslie and Slim or Dakota and Eileen, Carole Landis actually married Colonel Tom Wallace. Here the act of democratic love was no exaggeration.

By this time, critics were beginning to tire of films which lauded the efforts of Hollywood and its stars at war. The *New York Times* greeted news of the forthcoming *Four Jills and a Jeep* with a cynical headline: "Hollywood Pats Itself." When the film finally opened, Bosley Crowther agreed with this sentiment: "As a matter of fact, the whole picture has an exploitation tone. The question is whether the public will be impressed in the manner desired."[9] Even soldiers occasionally complained of Hollywood's pseudo-humility. A USO official noted: "Soldiers dislike being played down to, all the more when the offenders are the glamor names of Hollywood. Their chief abhorrence is the master of ceremonies who approaches them with, 'To you who are about to go forth into battle, we bring this modest tribute.' They can also do without repetitious salutes to their bravery and sacrifices."[10]

Yet, despite Hollywood's desire for self-congratulatory public relations, one fact must be remembered. Although fictional romances dot the Canteen films, the basic facts are unexaggerated. Hollywood and Broadway stars, as well as those behind the scenes, actively participated in USO tours, camp shows, and the formation of Canteens. The democratic and classless wartime society portrayed by these films was perhaps not as romantic as one might imagine.

PART SIX

PAST AND FUTURE

12

That Proustian Spirit

In 1943, when *Motion Picture Herald* queried theater own-ers about the pictures their audiences wanted to see, ex-hibitors clamored for "escapist films." Citing such musi-cals as *For Me and My Gal, Hello, Frisco, Hello,* and *Yankee Doodle Dandy* as crowd favorites, they claimed that the public was tiring of war films and merely wanted to for-get their problems for a few brief hours in a darkened theatre.[1] These three popular musicals seemingly filled the bill because they transported the viewer to an era prior to the troubled days of World War II. Nostalgia thus swiftly became one of the favorite genres of wartime Hollywood.

Variety noted the emergence of this trend as early as 1941:

Nostalgia is paying off plenty these days to those writers who are smart enough to turn to the "good old days" for material. At no time in the history of the industry have pro-ducers leaped with such enthusiasm to other times in the fashioning of their picture menus. With two-thirds of the world wallowing in war, the films now propose to turn back the clock to days when people were happier or thought they were.[2]

The *New York Times* similarly noted that "a Proustian spirit has been brooding over the creative acres of Hollywood, moving the souls of the Cinema Sanhedrin to 'the recapture of lost times' and revocation of days never to be lived again, save in the shadowland of one's favorite film theatre."[3]

Yet, despite the talk of escape to a calm and less-troubled world, Hollywood's musical nostalgia assumed a curious form during World War II. Although the majority of nostalgia films attempted to portray the past, they remained trapped in the present. No matter how far back in time the musical comedy traveled, it seemed unable to escape from the violence of the present day. No matter the studio, no matter the creators or stars, the nostalgic musical of the wartime period became almost a musical tragedy pervaded by death, violence, and mutilation. In this atmosphere the possibility of "escape" almost disappeared.

The Story of Vernon and Irene Castle, directed by H.C. Potter, the last of the Fred Astaire and Ginger Rogers musicals at RKO, revealed the difficulty of escaping from the world at war. Released before American entry into the conflict, this film at first attempts to capture the carefree spirit of the previous Astaire and Rogers' films. The number one dance team of the 1930s enacts the life of the Castles, whose Castle Walk swept America and the Continent before World War I. The early life of the Castles is treated in great detail from their meeting on a Coney Island beach to their years in Paris where they developed their classic dance style. In a spirited montage, the Castle rage is depicted by a stream of Castle endorsed products (dance shoes, bonbons, face cream, cigars) and even the Castle bob, Irene's personal hair style. The ultimate nature of their success is shown by a grand Castle Walk across a huge map of the United States.

The success, glory, and good spirits of the Castles' early years abruptly disappear as World War I begins and Great

Britain enters the war. Vernon, born in England, desires
to enlist but Irene, portraying the selfish wife, wishes him
to remain at home. Vernon appears at a benefit for the
Royal Flying Corps and sings, "It's a Long Way to Tipper-
ary" with the other enlisted men. He then refuses to take
a bow with the others because they have contributed so
much more than he to the war effort. Embarrassed, Vernon
enlists without telling Irene. He explains later: "Maybe if
America were in the war, you would understand why I
have to go."

Vernon flies dangerous spy missions over Germany,
while Irene foresakes her dancing career to sell Liberty
Bonds. After the United States enters the war ("That
means it's almost over," says Vernon), Vernon and Irene
move to Texas, where he teaches young Americans to fly
war planes. Vernon is killed on a training flight in a valiant
attempt to save the life of a young rookie. Irene hears the
news and collapses in her hotel room. A ghost of Vernon
appears, and they dance off into the clouds.

This is certainly a somber ending for a musical comedy,
especially such an excursion into the nostalgic past. The
plight of the Castles was no exception; the nostalgic musicals of the period seemed unable to escape the horrors and
personal dislocations of the war.

While RKO initiated this trend, Twentieth Century-Fox
capitalized on it. By the time *Tin Pan Alley* arrived in 1941,
Bosley Crowther identified the Fox formula as "music,
memory lane, plus heartbreak."[4] As the war progressed,
heartbreak became the novel element in this trend, and the
nostalgia that Fox produced after *Alexander's Ragtime Band*
became increasingly more bitter. Suddenly, Fox began presenting World War I musicals that really concerned World
War II.

By 1945, when *The Dolly Sisters* was released, the Fox formula had solidified at its most violent. Jenny (Betty Grable)

gives up the Folies Bergere to become the wife of Harvey
Fox (John Payne), who supposedly wrote "I'm Always
Chasing Rainbows" (actually composed by Joseph
McCarthy and Harry Carroll). Like Mrs. Castle, Jenny
withdraws from public life and performs only to sell Liberty Bonds. She is happy in a small Long Island home with
her beloved Harry. But one day Harry arrives home with
the news that he has enlisted:

JENNY: You did it!
HARRY: I had to—I sang at rallies and got other fellows
        to enlist. I'm in a new act now, the biggest act
        of all.

The Dolly Sisters return to Europe to perform as soon
as Harry leaves. Almost immediately the marriage begins
to collapse. As a group of soldiers sing "There Are Smiles
That Make You Happy," Harry sees a news photo of Jenny
cavorting with a duke. He returns to Paris and asks Jenny
to join him in Germany with the army of occupation. "I
can't keep up this long distance business forever. You have
to make a decision." She decides to remain in Paris and asks
Harry to stay. "I can't, I'm in the army, remember?" he replies. She begins to cry. Harry remarks coldly, "Save your
tears for the divorce court. They do you more good there."

The sister act breaks up soon afterward as Rosie (June
Haver) decides to marry a Chicago department store heir.
Jenny, steeped in despair, drives a car off a nearby cliff.
Harry, about to remarry, hears that she may be crippled
for life. He rushes to her bedside, where she is encased in
bandages. They eventually reconcile and remarry to the
tune of "I'm Always Chasing Rainbows." This may be a
happy ending, but it does little to alleviate the depressing
atmosphere of *The Dolly Sisters,* as the war once again
changed the lives of the protagonists in this so-called musical comedy.

M-G-M followed the trend initiated by RKO and Fox with Busby Berkeley's *For Me and My Gal* (1942). This tale of young vaudevillians anxious to play the Palace introduced Gene Kelly to the screen and gave Judy Garland her first star billing. Although the title cards explained that the film was dedicated to "the history of vaudeville," *For Me and My Gal* actually revealed the tensions of everyday life in a world at war.

In mid-1916 Harry Palmer (Kelly) meets Jimmy Metcalfe (George Murphy) and Jo Hayden (Judy Garland) while trouping through Iowa. Although the world is mobilizing for war, the innocent vaudevillians are blissfully unaware of such developments. Harry habitually scans the inside sections of the daily papers while the headlines read "Germans Reach Paris." Harry is more interested in convincing Jo to join him in a vaudeville team. He offers her a new song, "For Me and My Gal," and she joins his act.

Harry and Jo eventually realize their love for each other and plan to marry after they play the Palace. Meanwhile, the dislocations of war come closer. Danny (Richard Quine), Jo's brother, quits medical school to enlist in the army. A nightclub audience sings him a teary good-bye with "Till We Meet Again."

Finally Palmer and Hayden receive the good news—they are booked into the Palace. Moments later Harry receives a second telegram, this one from Uncle Sam. Harry learns that he is to be drafted, and he is furious: "Do you think that anything will stand in the way of us playing the Palace this time. Not even a war! I'll beat this." Jo is bewildered by his attitude, as she stares at a photo of her brother Danny in uniform.

Harry the hoofer decides he can sacrifice a hand in order to get out of the army. After some soul-searching he crushes his hand in the trunk he was born in and gets a six-week delay from his draft board. When he receives word of the postponement, he returns to tell Jo the good news.

Unbeknownst to Harry, in a surprisingly short interval, Jimmy Metcalf has enlisted and Jo's brother Danny has been killed in action. This is timing at its worst. Harry tells Jo that "he did it for them," but she is revolted and says she "never wants to see him again as long as she lives—never!"

Harry repents and tries to enlist, but no branch of the service will take him once they discover his hand has been permanently mutilated. He realizes he did "the worst thing in the world" and all his friends shun him. Meanwhile, Harry discovers his friend Sid Sims (Ben Blue) singing "What Are You Going to Do to Help the Boys?" at a Liberty Bond rally. Sims convinces him to join the YMCA troupe and come to France to entertain the boys.

Harry meets Jo once again in Paris where she, too, is entertaining the troops. She is cold and aloof, but all Harry wants to hear is "that he is not a coward." Jo replies that she doesn't hate him, and they part once again. Months afterward, Harry saves a convoy of ambulances from a German ambush and is awarded a distinguished service medal.

After the war, Harry returns to New York and discovers that Jo is playing the Palace alone. Jo spots Harry and his medal in the audience, and they are reunited on the Palace stage where they perform "For Me and My Gal."

This is certainly a happy ending, but the path is strewn with heartbreak, mutilation, and death, hardly the prime ingredients for a musical comedy. However, any musical recalling a war had to present the tragedy as well as the glory.

In order for nostalgia to truly escape from unpleasant realities, producers had to look for subjects which avoided periods of strife, conflict, or war. Thus, *Meet Me in St. Louis*, based on the stories of Sally Benson, seemed an ideal adventure into a golden past for nostalgia buffs. *Meet Me In St.*

Louis (1944) managed to do what other nostalgic musicals had attempted but failed. This Arthur Freed-Vincente Minnelli musical avoided the war that had soured the plots of other musical comedies. *Meet Me in St. Louis* became a trip into the family photo album. There was to be no war or bloodshed. The simple plot concerned an amiable family that is about to move to New York. The most momentous question raised is whether Esther (Judy Garland) will marry the boy next door.

But within this tranquil past a curious trouble is brewing. The wholesomeness of this world of yesteryear sours when it is seen though the eyes of Tootie (Margaret O'Brien), the youngest family member, who is most disturbed by the move to New York. Her violent and psychologically upsetting vision disrupts the placid world of turn-of-the-century St. Louis.

The Halloween sequence is particularly violent. The children wander the streets in unruly mobs, burning piles of leaves. "Kill them all!" shout the children as they speak of the evil adults. "Burn down their houses—burn the soles of their feet!" Tootie becomes the leader of this motley gang, since she volunteers to confront the evil Brockoff. The youths believe this neighbor poisons their cats and incinerates them in his furnace. Brockoff faints, and Tootie thinks she has murdered him. She becomes a hero to the others. "I am the most horrible," she proclaims. The stark images of mobs, burnings, torture, and murder seem to recall Nazi Germany more than the golden days of old St. Louis.

By Christmas time, Tootie's tragic vision of life turns even bleaker. She kills the snowpeople in the backyard which represent her family and friends. She decides to behead these statues rather than leave them behind. Judy Garland eventually manages to calm her by singing "Have Yourself a Merry Little Christmas" and urges her to look to the future when she may once again be happy. The father (Leon Ames) finally realizes that his family would be happier in St. Louis, so he turns down the job offer from New York.

Once again the nostalgic musical offers a happy ending, but only after a sequence of violence and psychological turmoil. To get an idea of the pessimistic tone of Judy's final number, it should be recalled that the original lyrics read "Have yourself a merry little Christmas . . . it may be your last." That "obviously wouldn't do" Minnelli recalled, as Esther was trying to comfort Tootie, not depress her even more.[5]

The past provided no refuge for a war-weary world. The creators of nostalgic musicals soon discovered that escape was impossible. The remembrance of life in the early part of the twentieth century provided little solace for World War II audiences.

13

Youth on Parade

The hope of the Nazi party remained the youth of Germany. Leni Riefenstahl's *Triumph of the Will* (1936), a frightening documentary of the 1934 Nuremberg Party Convention, presented the healthy, scrubbed children of the Rhineland as devoted and enthusiastic followers of Adolf Hitler. No matter the age, these youngsters seemed to possess a political fidelity which would assure conquest by the master race. The Hitler youth appeared on film as a vivid testimony of the strength of Nazi principles throughout Germany.

American film-makers assumed a considerably more jaundiced view of these incipient politicos. From Hollywood's vantage point, the youth's devotion to the German State subverted the American ideal of home and family. In that totalitarian setting, parents even began to fear their own children. In *Hitler's Children* (1941), the elderly Dr. Schmidt is forced to speak in a whisper lest his children overhear his conversation with an American school teacher. All family loyalty is sacrificed to the sovereignty of the state. Even love, that most sacred of emotions, disappears within Hollywood's version of the Third Reich. For example, Robert Young, a youthful party

member, is forced to kill Margaret Sullavan, his former
girlfriend, as she tries to flee to Switzerland in *The Mortal
Storm* (1941).

While American screenwriters depicted the Nazi youth
as cold and calculating, they began to wonder about the
role of American youth. Hitler had organized the German
kinder into a vital political force, but what had American
society done to encourage the support of its youth for the
war effort?

American audiences need not have worried. From the
early days of the war in Europe, the Hollywood musical
presented the domestic counterpart of the Hitler Youth.
These musical *wunderkind* were as politically active as their
German counterparts. They staunchly supported American intervention and participation in the European war.
As the German youth admired Hitler, American youth
idolized Franklin Delano Roosevelt. They maintained a
firm belief in the rectitude of their own actions and their
ability to dominate any adverse situation. But, most important, these American youths displayed a reverence for emotion and family ties that their German counterparts lacked.
Love, honor, fidelity, nobility, and friendship surpassed all
other goals. The state thus had no influence over devotion
to home, family, and friends.

The leaders of this American musical youth movement
were none other than Mickey Rooney and Judy Garland
in a series of M-G-M films directed by Busby Berkeley.
Babes in Arms (1939), *Strike Up the Band* (1940), and *Babes on
Broadway* (1941) presented a concerned and politically active youth vitally interested in American wartime efforts.
These films have rarely been discussed in terms of their
political content; usually they are considered as exten-
sions of Busby Berkeley's backstage musicals at Warner's
in the 1930s. Yet, while Warner Brothers musicals were
steeped in Depression myths and New Deal ideology, the

Garland-Rooney films expressed the political concerns of contemporary American society in the period before Pearl Harbor.

In all of these films, American youth becomes the hope of the future. *Babes in Arms,* a loose adaptation of a 1937 Rodgers and Hart stage musical, begins in the midst of the Depression. Vaudeville is dying, due to the onslaught of the motion picture and the dire economic situation. As the aging vaudevillians ponder their unemployment, they decide to take to the road once again and revive their prosperous stage show of the early twenties. The children want to assist their parents, but the elders prefer that their children stay in school so they might become doctors or lawyers.

Michael Z. Moran (Mickey Rooney) rebels when he hears his parents' plans. He decides that children are also capable of presenting a show. The youthful performers march through the town to a local barn. They build a bonfire, light torches, and sing "Babes in Arms," which acquires a curiously martial air in this atmosphere. The song almost becomes a war cry:

> They call us babes in arms,
> But we're babies in armor.
> They laugh at babes in arms,
> But we'll be laughing far more.
> On city streets and farms
> They'll hear a rising war cry.
> Youth will arrive
> Let them know you're alive.
> Make it your cry.
> Play day is done
> We've a place in the sun
> We must fight for.
> So babes in arms—
> To arms!

As the group gathers around the bonfire, Douglas Mac-
Phail perverts the melody of a Wagnerian interlude and
sings of the future:

> It's a new day
> Our flag's unfurled
> C'mon, let's tell it to the world.*

After their collective identity is established, the "babes"
begin work.

While the parents' vaudeville show is a dismal failure,
the youths succeed beyond their wildest dreams. A producer sees the show in the country barn and offers to bring
it to Broadway. As in all the Garland and Rooney films,
a successful show is the result, but it is not the only goal.
Far more important than a Broadway hit is the unity of the
group. Friendship means more to these children than financial or critical success.

The emphasis on group unity can be seen in all of these
films. In *Babes in Arms,* Pat (Judy Garland) threatens to
leave the show because she is replaced by Baby Rosalie, a
child star who agrees to bankroll the endeavor. Pat visits
her mother on the road in Buffalo. Pat's mom explains:
"You shouldn't have done it. Michael cast Baby Rosalie for
everyone's benefit. You never walk out on a show." Pat decides she's no quitter and returns to the show.

Mickey Rooney faces a similar problem in *Strike Up the
Band.* After practicing with a local swing band for several
months, Mickey receives an offer to join Paul Whiteman's
band as a drummer in New York City. His mother also explains: "Everyone's been working so hard—working for
the whole group, and you'll be walking out on your
friends." Mickey accepts his mother's advice and leads his

---

*"Babes in Arms," by Rodgers & Hart. Copyright © 1937 by Chappell & Co., Inc. Copy-
right renewed. International copyright secured. All rights reserved. Used by permission.

band to a successful show in a national competition. In *Babes on Broadway*, Mickey faces yet another moral problem. He pretends sympathy for a group of British war orphans, but only intends to use them to gain funds for a future show. Judy learns Mickey's true sentiments and berates his insincerity. Mickey then begins to question his values and eventually gives his support to the orphans' fund for summer camp.

Friends and family are thus more important than success in show business in these films. When young Willie needs an operation in *Strike Up the Band*, Mickey willingly donates two hundred dollars for a chartered flight to a medical center, even though he had been saving the money for the band's bus fare to the Chicago contest. Similarly, in *Babes in Arms*, Mickey refuses to put his show on Broadway until his father is given a job in the show so that his faith in his own ability can be restored. Parents provide the inspiration for the children's success, even if they are unable to participate actively. Although Mickey and his band have practiced for months, it is his mother who deserves the praise at the big contest: "Thanks to the most important of all—Mom. She's a queen."

While the plots of these musicals concentrate on the importance of group unity in times of stress, the musical numbers present undying praise for Roosevelt and the American war effort. The "big show" at the end of each film becomes a symbolic display of youth's support for the United States. As Mickey explains in *Babes in Arms:* "I'm proving to all the kids that there's an American dream—it's bigger than a show—it's the entire country."

Each succeeding musical comments on the political events at the time of its production. Although *Babes in Arms* takes place in 1931, the songs seem more reflective of 1939. First Mickey and Judy sing Harold Arlen and E.Y. Harburg's "God's Country," where "smiles are broader and freedom's greater; and every man is his own dictator." The performers do not sing this song from the stage, but walk among the members of the audience, as though to convince them of this musical evocation of the merits of American democracy. In a pointed reference to the current international situation, Mickey and Judy solemnly add:

> All of you who think it's so much easier to give in
> Count your many blessings in this wondrous land we live in.

After this song, Mickey and Judy impersonate the heroes of this series of musical films. Mickey becomes Franklin Delano Roosevelt at a fireside chat, and Judy mimics Eleanor Roosevelt in a recitation of "My Day." They then dance with representatives of labor unions, foreign ambassadors, and minority groups on the stairs of the White House. The finale becomes a melodic summary of foreign policy:

> We send our greetings to friendly nations
> We may be Yanks, but we're your relations
> Drop your sabres
> We're all going to be Good Neighbors
> In God's country.*

By 1940, *Strike Up the Band* assumed a more militant stand. The title song had to be wholly revised in order to be appropriate in the political climate of the time.

> We hope there'll be no other war,
> But if we are forced into one—
> The flag that we'll be fighting for
> Is the Red and White and Blue one!†

While *Babes in Arms* hinted at pacifism, and *Strike Up the Band* assumed a militant stand, *Babes on Broadway* faced a declining situation in Europe. Here the key issue becomes the safety of war orphans from Britain. Judy Garland sings "Chin Up, Cheerio, Carry On" at a rally for the children:

> From the dark cafes of Paris,
> From the streets of Amsterdam,
> From the homes of old Vienna,
> To the shores of Uncle Sam.
> Wherever freedom's hope is true,
> Each heart cries out to you.
> Don't give up Tommy Atkins,
> Be a stout fellow,
> Chin up, Cheerio, Carry On!
> Keep a stiff upper lip,
> When in doubt fellow,
> Chin Up, Cherrio, Carry On!
> Oh, the sun's sure to smile,
> On your bright little isle.
> So hang on to your wits,
> And we'll turn the blitz on Fritz!*

While the threat of war remained abstract in the earlier films, *Babes on Broadway* presents the war with an unstinting realism. Images of war-torn London accompany Judy's song. The empty streets and bombed buildings are superimposed over the orphans' faces. They begin to cry as they recall their former tranquil life.

Once again Roosevelt is the hero in this film. He is referred to passingly in "How About You" ("and Franklin Roosevelt's looks give me a thrill") and is adulated in the minstrel show number "Franklin D. Roosevelt Jones," a Harold Rome song lifted from the Broadway show, *Sing*

---

*"Chin Up, Cheerio, Carry On" by E. Y. Harburg and Burton Lane. Copyright © 1941, renewed 1969 Metro-Goldwyn-Mayer Inc. All rights administered by Leo Feist, Inc. All rights reserved. Used by permission.

Out the News (1938). Dressed in blackface, Mickey and Judy sing of a recently born black child named after the great American leader ("When he grows up, he'll never stray, with a name like he's got today—Just wait and see, he'll make history.")

Mickey Rooney and Judy Garland split up after *Babes on Broadway* to pursue their own careers. They were reunited briefly in 1943 in an adaptation of George and Ira Gershwin's *Girl Crazy*, a 1930 Broadway musical. Although Arthur Freed produced once again, the rest of the creative talent from the earlier films had disappeared. Busby Berkeley directed only the "I Got Rhythm" finale, Charles Walters directed Judy Garland's solo numbers, and Norman Taurog directed the rest of the film. As a result, *Girl Crazy* lacks any unity with the earlier films. Unlike *Babes in Arms*, *Girl Crazy* relies heavily on its Broadway progenitor, and consequently all concern with the themes and political persuasion of the earlier films is lost. Even here Judy and Mickey initially are not friends, but antagonists. Perhaps the lack of political concern is a result of the film's late date, long after America's entry in the war. Hence, while the pre-Pearl Harbor films faced the problem of providing a rationale for American entry into the war, *Girl Crazy* was released after American intervention had become fact.

The Mickey Rooney and Judy Garland musicals are far more than rehashes of the "backstage musical" theme, as the recent compendium *That's Entertainment* seemed to imply. These films presented a committed American youth faithful to their country's leaders and foreign policy. As World War II has passed into history, the likes of these patriotic musicals will, no doubt, rarely be seen again.

14

Conclusion: Demobilization and Peacetime

By 1939 the musical comedy had almost disappeared from American screens. World War II revived the musical and gave it a sense of mission. It became streamlined in form and committed to the task of winning the war in the hearts and minds of the American people. Audiences responded to this patriotic message and flocked to see almost four hundred musical films during the wartime era.

Peace killed the musical comedy boom. During 1944, seventy-six film musicals were released; by 1950, only twenty-two. At the present time the number of musicals can be counted on the finger(s) of one hand. What caused Hollywood's most popular film genre to almost vanish?

The key to the success of the wartime musical was topicality. Escapism was shunned as writers, composers, lyricists, and stars addressed themselves to the problems of a society at war. With the coming of peace, Hollywood had to discover new themes and formats for the musical which would be relevant to postwar audiences.

The creators of the musical film were unable to respond to a society at peace with the same speed and fervor that

161

they reacted to a society at war. Instead, the musical relied on standard formulas of the war years which had little meaning after 1945. One of the best examples of this cultural lag concerns the continuation of "soldier musicals" for almost ten years after the war's end. For Hollywood the war seemingly ended in 1955. Until then, musical soldiers dominated such films as *Tars and Spars* (1946), *On an Island with You* (1948), *On the Town* (1949), *The West Point Story* (1950), *G. I. Jane* (1951), and *Three Sailors and a Girl* (1953). Finally, *It's Always Fair Weather* (1955) brought the soldiers home for a peacetime reunion.

Only M-G-M brought some relief from these war-in-peacetime musical films. With such films as *An American in Paris* (1951), *Singin' in the Rain* (1952), and *The Bandwagon* (1953), producer Arthur Freed encouraged experimentation with musical forms. By 1960, a money crunch curtailed Freed's independence, and the brief golden age of the M-G-M musical came to an end. Although M-G-M dedicated *That's Entertainment* to the illustrious Freed, the studio had dismissed him years earlier. For M-G-M, the musical was dead.

By 1960, all experimentation had ended. Hollywood abandoned its traditional role as a producer of musicals equal in quality to those of Broadway. Now films merely duplicated Broadway originals with such films as *Damn Yankees* (1958), *Bells Are Ringing* (1960), *Gypsy, Jumbo, The Music Man* (all 1962), and *Bye Bye Birdie* (1963). With few exceptions, these film adaptations added little to the stage versions. The scale of the enterprise may have expanded, but script, music, and performances remained almost the same as they had been on Broadway.

The outstanding success of *The Sound of Music* in 1965 brought some hope that audiences might be interested in musicals once again. Yet, such costly flops as *Camelot* (1967), *Hello Dolly* (1969), *Man of La Mancha* (1972), and *Mame* (1974), followed soon after.

What hope is there? Can the musical ever achieve its former glory? One lesson might be learned from the wartime musicals. While it has been generally assumed that a musical must be escapist in form, the wartime musical showed that relevance was the key to success. Films that utilized modern music and contemporary themes achieved the greatest popularity. This is the message that current directors of musical films seem to be ignoring. Peter Bogdanovich's *At Long Last Love* (1975) attempted to revive the Astaire and Rogers musicals; Ken Russell's *The Boy Friend* (1971) returned to the days of Busby Berkeley; and Martin Scorsese's *New York, New York* (1977) recalled the "soldier musicals" of the 1940s.

The film musical is not a dead art form. Classics need not be continually revived or copied. Musicals featuring contemporary themes and music have the greatest opportunity for success. The "rock musicals" *Hair, Jesus Christ Superstar,* and *Godspell* drew Broadway audiences because they introduced modern music to the musical comedy stage at a time when other shows were mimicking Rodgers and Hammerstein. Reusing images of past forms has stultified the growth of the musical comedy both in Hollywood and on Broadway. Only change can save it now.

Notes

INTRODUCTION

1. Roy Paul Madsen, *The Impact of Film* (New York, 1973), p. 308.
2. Andrew Bergman, *We're in the Money* (New York, 1974).

CHAPTER 1

1. *Variety*, September 18, 1940, p. 3. For the role of motion pictures during World War II, see: Richard R. Lingeman, *Don't You Know There's a War On?* (New York, 1970), and Robert Sklar, *Movie Made America* (New York, 1975), ch. 15.
2. All quotes are from *Moving Picture Screen and Radio Propaganda*, Subcommittee of the Committee on Interstate Commerce, September 23, 1941.
3. See William Stott, *Documentary Expression and Thirties America* (New York, 1973).
4. "Hollywood in Uniform," *Fortune* (April 1942), pp. 92–95.
5. Gregory D. Black and Clayton R. Koppes, "OWI Goes to the Movies: The Bureau of Intelligence's Criticism of Hollywood," *Prologue* (Spring 1974), p. 48. See also John Morton Blum, *V Was for Victory* (New York, 1976) and Allan M. Winkler, *The Politics of Propaganda. The Office of War Information, 1942–1945* (New Haven, 1978) for further information on the OWI.

6. Garth Jowett, *Film, The Democratic Art* (Boston, 1976), pp. 307–9.
7. "Hollywood Counts the Pennies," *New York Times Magazine* (August 30, 1942), p. 15.

CHAPTER 2

1. Mervyn LeRoy, interview, *Today Show*, March 22, 1974.
2. *New York Times*, October 29, 1939.
3. Miles Kreuger, *The Movie Musical* (New York, 1975), pp. ix-xi.
4. Arlene Croce, *The Fred Astaire and Ginger Rogers Book* (London, 1972).
5. See Richard Rodgers, *Musical Stages* (New York, 1975), ch. 12.

CHAPTER 3

1. *Variety*, December 28, 1938, p. 1.
2. Ibid., September 21, 1938; September 13, 1939.
3. Ibid., November 30, 1938.
4. *New York Times*, July 10, 1938.
5. Ibid.
6. Ibid., April 25, 1937.
7. *Variety*, February 23, 1939.
8. Eleanor Knowles, *The Films of Jeanette MacDonald and Nelson Eddy* (New York, 1975), p.p. 253–60.
9. Hugh Fordin, *The World of Entertainment* (New York, 1975), p. 43.

CHAPTER 4

1. Jack L. Warner, *My First Hundred Years In Hollywood* (New York, 1964), pp. 261–62.
2. *New York Times*, January 10, 1943.
3. Ibid., March 1, May 4, 6, 7, July 14, August 14, 1942.
4. *Motion Picture Herald*, July 31, 1943.
5. *Variety*, July 14, 1943.
6. Robert Kimball, *Cole* (New York, 1971), p. 134.
7. *New York Times*, July 17, 1945.

CHAPTER 5

1. *New York Times,* June 19, 1941.
2. Ibid.
3. For discussions of the OWI, see Sidney Weinberg, "What to Tell America: The Writers' Quarrel with the OWI," *Journal of American History* (June 1968); Gregory D. Black and Clayton R. Koppes, "OWI Goes to the Movies: The Bureau of Intelligence's Criticism of Hollywood, 1942–43," *Prologue* (Spring 1974), pp. 44–59.
4. *Variety,* October 7, 1942, p. 2.
5. Ibid.
6. *New York Times,* July 11, 14, 1940.
7. See: *Variety,* October 2, 1940, for the origin of *Yip Yip Yaphank.*
8. For the origins of this show, see Max Wilk, *They're Playing Our Song* (New York, 1973), pp. 286–88.
9. Ira Gershwin, *Lyrics on Several Occasions* (New York, 1973), pp. 224–27; and, Robert Kimball and Alfred Simon, *The Gershwins* (New York, 1973), p. 119.
10. *Variety,* May 5, 1940.
11. Ibid., May 26, 1943.
12. *New York Times Magazine,* June 6, 1943, p. 31.
13. *New York Times,* June 9, 1941.
14. Ibid., November 4, 1941.
15. Ibid., January 14, 1942.
16. For a discussion of *Holiday Inn,* see Stanley Green and Burt Goldblatt, *Starring Fred Astaire* (New York, 1973), pp. 230–43.
17. Lingeman, *Don't You Know There's a War On?,* p. 214.
18. Michael Freedland, *Irving Berlin* (New York, 1974), p. 148.

CHAPTER 7

1. *Variety,* September 18, 1940.
2. Ibid.
3. Hugh Fordin, *The World of Entertainment* (New York, 1975), p. 66.
4. *For Me and My Gal* is discussed in greater detail in chapter 12.

5. *New York Times,* December 17, 1944.
6. Ibid., June 17, 1945.

CHAPTER 9

1. Such films as *The Greaser's Gauntlet* (1908) and *Tony the Greaser* (1911) were indicative of this attitude. See Allen Woll, *The Latin Image in American Film, 1894–1976* (UCLA, 1977), ch. 1.
2. See Russ Merritt, *Marquee Theatre* (Madison, Wis., 1971), p. 17.
3. Quoted in Bryce Wood, *The Making of the Good Neighbor Policy* (New York, 1961), pp. 130–31.
4. For a history of this office, see Donald W. Rowland (comp.), *History of the Office of the Coordinator of Inter-American Affairs* (Washington, D. C., 1947).
5. *Film Daily Yearbook of Motion Pictures* (1943), p. 47.
6. *Variety,* April 2, 1941.
7. Orson Welles' *It's All True,* a joint venture with RKO, was one of the Division's most renowned failures. See Joseph McBride, *Orson Welles* (New York, 1973).
8. *Motion Picture Herald,* January 10, 1942.
9. *Politics,* July 1945, p. 211.
10. *Motion Picture Herald,* April 11, 1942.
11. *Variety,* February 19, 1941.
12. Ibid., June 25, 1941.
13. For an explanation of this practice, see *The Nation,* February 15, 1941, p. 193.
14. *Newsweek,* July 22, 1940, p. 12.
15. *Variety,* November 6, 1940.
16. Ibid., March 20, 1940.
17. Quoted in Ted Sennett, *Warner Brothers Presents* (New York, 1971), p. 280.
18. *New York Times,* April 30, 1939, IX, p. 5.
19. Ibid., April 23, 1939, X, p. 4. The other writers were John Huston and Wolfgang Reinhardt.
20. *New York Times,* July 2, 1939, X, p. 4.
21. *Variety,* December 27, 1939.
22. *Time,* November 9, 1942.

23. *New York Post,* November 30, 1955.
24. *Etude,* October 1941.
25. See Tony Thomas and Jim Terry, *The Busby Berkeley Book* (New York, 1973), pp. 152–54.
26. *Variety,* October 9, 1940.
27. Ibid., October 8, 1941.
28. Ibid., June 4, 1941.
29. Ibid., November 6, 1940.
30. *O Imparcial* (Rio de Janeiro, Brazil), August 22, 1940.
31. *Variety,* November 6, 1940, p. 3.
32. *Sintonia* (Buenos Aires, Argentina), June 11, 1941.
33. *Variety,* June 25, 1941, pp. 3, 34.
34. Ibid., December 19, 1945.
35. Ibid.
36. Ibid., February 27, 1946.

CHAPTER 10

1. *New York Times,* February 7, 1943. For recent studies of the black image in American film, see Thomas Cripps, *Slow Fade to Black* (New York, 1977); Donald Bogle, *Toms, Coons, Mulattoes, Mammies, and Bucks* (New York, 1974); and Daniel Leab, *From Sambo to Superspade* (Boston, 1975).
2. *New Republic,* July 5, 1943.
3. *New York Times,* February 7, 1943.

CHAPTER 11

1. *Photoplay,* June 1942, p. 62.
2. Ibid., p. 31.
3. *New York Times,* February 7, 1942.
4. Ibid., March 3, 1942.
5. *Theatre Arts,* April 1943, p. 229.
6. *Variety,* January 13, 1943.
7. Ibid., September 8, 1943.
8. *New York Times,* November 21, 1944.
9. W. Franklyn Mosher, *The Alice Faye Movie Book* (Harrisburg, Pa., 1974), pp. 169–70.
10. *New York Times,* March 1, 1942.

CHAPTER 12

1. *Motion Picture Herald*, May 8, 1943, p. 13.
2. *Variety*, July 16, 1941.
3. *New York Times*, May 5, 1940.
4. Ibid., November 24, 1940.
5. Vincente Minnelli, *I Remember It Well* (New York, 1974), p. 138.

Filmography

I would like to thank the following individuals and institutions for supplying prints of the films discussed in this book. Susan Dalton and the staff of the University of Wisconsin Center for Theatre Research provided access to all the RKO and Warner Brothers films. Thomas O'Brien, Sr. and Thomas O'Brien, Jr., graciously provided several Columbia musicals for my viewing. The Library of Congress Film Division and Films Incorporated of Skokie, Illinois, allowed me to view the M-G-M films that I have discussed.

1939   *Babes in Arms* (M-G-M)
       Broadway Serenade (M-G-M)
       Let Freedom Ring (M-G-M)
       Naughty But Nice (Warner Bros.)
       The Story of Vernon and Irene Castle (RKO)
       That's Right, You're Wrong (RKO)
       The Wizard of Oz (M-G-M)

1940   *Bitter Sweet* (M-G-M)
       Broadway Melody (M-G-M)
       Dance Girl Dance (RKO)
       The New Moon (M-G-M)
       One Night in the Tropics (Universal)
       Second Chorus (Paramount)

Strike Up the Band (M-G-M)
Tin Pan Alley (Twentieth Century-Fox)
Too Many Girls (RKO)
Young People (Twentieth Century-Fox)

1941   *Babes on Broadway* (M-G-M)
       Blues in the Night (Warner Bros.)
       Buck Privates (Universal)
       The Chocolate Soldier (M-G-M)
       Four Jacks and a Jill (RKO)
       Lady Be Good (M-G-M)
       Moon Over Miami (Twentieth Century-Fox)
       Navy Blues (Warner Bros.)
       Sun Valley Serenade (Twentieth Century-Fox)
       That Night in Rio (Twentieth Century-Fox)
       They Met in Argentina (RKO)
       Weekend in Havana (Twentieth Century-Fox)
       You'll Never Get Rich (Columbia)
       Ziegfeld Girl (M-G-M)

1942   *Footlight Serenade* (Twentieth Century-Fox)
       For Me and My Gal (M-G-M)
       Holiday Inn (Paramount)
       I Married an Angel (M-G-M)
       Mayor of 44th Street (RKO)
       Orchestra Wives (Twentieth Century-Fox)
       Rhythm Parade (Monogram)
       Rio Rita (M-G-M)
       Seven Days Leave (RKO)
       Springtime in the Rockies (Twentieth Century-Fox)
       Star Spangled Rhythm (Paramount)
       Yankee Doodle Dandy (Warner Bros.)
       You Were Never Lovelier (Columbia)

1943   *Best Foot Forward* (M-G-M)
       Cabin in the Sky (M-G-M)
       The Desert Song (Warner Bros.)

The Gang's All Here (Twentieth Century-Fox)
Girl Crazy (M-G-M)
Higher and Higher (RKO)
Hit the Ice (Universal)
I Dood It (M-G-M)
Presenting Lily Mars (M-G-M)
The Sky's the Limit (RKO)
Something to Shout About (Columbia)
Stage Door Canteen (United Artists)
Stormy Weather (Twentieth Century-Fox)
Thank Your Lucky Stars (Warner Bros.)
This Is the Army (Warner Bros.)
Thousands Cheer (M-G-M)

1944   *Bathing Beauty* (M-G-M)
Broadway Rhythm (M-G-M)
Cover Girl (Columbia)
Four Jills in a Jeep (RKO)
Hey Rookie (Columbia)
Hollywood Canteen (Warner Bros.)
Lady in the Dark (Paramount)
Louisiana Hayride (Republic)
Meet Me in St. Louis (M-G-M)
Meet the People (M-G-M)
Rosie the Riveter (Republic)
Seven Days Ashore (RKO)
Show Business (RKO)
Song of the Open Road (United Artists)
Step Lively (RKO)
Two Girls and a Sailor (M-G-M)
Up in Arms (RKO)

1945   *Anchors Aweigh* (M-G-M)
The Dolly Sisters (Twentieth Century-Fox)
George White's Scandals of 1945 (RKO)
Pan-Americana (RKO)
Rhapsody in Blue (Warner Bros.)

State Fair (Twentieth Century-Fox)
Thrill of a Romance (M-G-M)
Yolanda and the Thief (M-G-M)

Bibliography

I would like to thank the staffs of the following archives for providing access to reviews, clippings, film stills, and press books of the films discussed herein: The Billy Rose Collection of the New York Public Library, the Museum of the City of New York, the Theater Collection of the Philadelphia Free Library, the Museum of Modern Art Film Stills Archive, and the University of Wisconsin Center for Theater Research.

Bergman, Andrew. *We're in the Money.* New York: New York University Press, 1971.

Bergman, Mark. "Hollywood in the Forties—Revisited." *Velvet Light Trap,* 5 (Summer 1972), pp. 2–5.

Black, Gregory D., and Clayton R. Koppes. "OWI Goes to the Movies: The Bureau of Intelligence's Criticism of Hollywood." *Prologue* (Spring 1974), pp. 48–64.

Blum, John Morton. *V Was for Victory.* New York: Harcourt Brace Jovanovich, 1976.

Bogle, Donald. *Toms, Coons, Mulattoes, Mammies, and Bucks.* New York: Viking, 1973.

Cripps, Thomas. *Slow Fade to Black.* New York: Oxford University Press, 1977.

Croce, Arlene. *The Fred Astaire and Ginger Rogers Book.* New York: Dutton, 1972.

Fordin, Hugh. *The World of Entertainment: The Freed Unit at MGM.* New York: Doubleday, 1975.

Freedland, Michael. *Irving Berlin.* New York: Stein and Day, 1974.

Gershwin, Ira. *Lyrics on Several Occasions.* New York: Viking Press, 1973.

Green, Stanley. *Starring Fred Astaire.* New York: Dodd, Mead, 1973.

Harmetz, Aljean. *The Making of "The Wizard of Oz."* New York: Knopf, 1977.

Haskell, Molly. *From Reverence to Rape.* New York: Holt, Rinehart, and Winston, 1973.

Higham, Charles, and Joel Greenberg. *Hollywood in the Forties.* New York: Paperback Library, 1970.

Hodgkinson, Anthony W. " 'Forty-Second Street' New Deal: Some Thoughts about Early Film Musicals." *Journal of Popular Film,* 4 (1975), pp. 33–46.

Jacobs, Lewis. "World War II and the American Film." *Cinema Journal,* 7 (Winter 1967–68), pp. 1–21.

Jones, Dorothy B. "The Hollywood War Film, 1942–1944." *Hollywood Quarterly,* 1 (October 1945), pp. 1–19.

Jowett, Garth. *Film: The Democratic Art.* Boston: Little, Brown, 1976.

Kimball, Robert. *Cole.* New York: Holt, Rinehart, and Winston, 1971.

Kimball, Robert, and Alfred Simon. *The Gershwins.* New York: Atheneum, 1973.

Knowles, Eleanor. *The Films of Jeanette MacDonald and Nelson Eddy.* New York: A. S. Barnes, 1975.

Krueger, Miles. *The Movie Musical from Vitaphone to "42nd Street."* New York: Dover, 1975.

Landrum, Larry N. "World War II in the Movies: A Selected Bibliography of Sources." *Journal of Popular Film,* 1 (Spring 1972), pp. 147–53.

Leab, Daniel. *From Sambo to Superspade.* Boston: Houghton Mifflin, 1975.

Lingeman, Richard R. *Don't You Know There's a War On?* New York: G. P. Putnam's, 1970.

Look Magazine, ed. *Movie Lot to Beachhead.* New York: Doubleday, Doran, 1945.

Madsen, Roy Paul. *The Impact of Film.* New York: MacMillan, 1973.

McClure, Arthur F. "Hollywood at War: The American Motion Picture and World War II, 1939–1945." *Journal of Popular Film,* 1 (Spring 1972), pp. 123–35.

Mellen, Joan. *Women and Their Sexuality in the New Film.* New York: Horizon Press, 1973.

Minnelli, Vincente. *I Remember It Well.* New York: Doubleday, 1974.

Mosher, W. Franklyn. *The Alice Faye Movie Book.* Harrisburg, Pa.: Stackpole Books, 1974.

Moving Picture Screen and Radio Propaganda. Subcommittee of the Committee on Interstate Commerce. Washington, D.C.: Government Printing Office, 1941.

Nugent, Frank S. "Hollywood Counts the Pennies." *New York Times Magazine,* August 30, 1942.

Perrett, Geoffrey. *Days of Sadness, Years of Triumph. The American People, 1939–1945.* New York: Coward, McCann, and Geoghegan, 1973.

Rodgers, Richard. *Musical Stages.* New York: Random House, 1975.

Rosen, Marjorie. *Popcorn Venus.* New York: Coward, McCann, and Geoghegan, 1973.

Roth, Mark. "Some Warner Musicals and the Spirit of the New Deal." *Velvet Light Trap,* 1 (June 1971), pp. 20–25.

Rowland, Donald W. *History of the Office of Inter-American Affairs.* Washington, D. C.: Government Printing Office, 1947.

Scheurer, Timothy E. "The Aesthetics of Form and Convention in the Movie Musical." *Journal of Popular Film,* 3 (1974), pp. 307–34.

Sennett, Ted. *Warner Brothers Presents.* New York: Castle Books, 1971.

Sklar, Robert. *Movie-Made America.* New York: Random House, 1976.

Thomas, Tony, and Jim Terry. *The Busby Berkeley Book.* New York: New York Graphic Society, 1973.

Warner, Jack L. *My First Hundred Years in Hollywood.* New York: Random House, 1964.

Weinberg, Sidney. "What to Tell America. The Writers' Quarrel with the OWI." *Journal of American History* (June 1968).

Wilk, Max. *They're Playing Our Song.* New York: Atheneum, 1973.

Woll, Allen L. *Songs From Hollywood Musical Comedies, 1927 to the Present: A Dictionary.* New York: Garland Press, 1976.

Woll, Allen L. *The Latin Image in American Film.* Los Angeles: UCLA Latin American Series, 1977.

Index

179

LEARNING RESOURCES

CENTER

ILLINOIS CENTRAL COLLEGE
MCMLXVI

East Peoria, Illinois